KT-559-168

BRISTOL CITY LIBRARIES

WITHDRAWN AND OFFERED FOR SALE

BSAL

Please return/renew this item by the last date shown
on this label, or on your self-service receipt.

To renew this item, visit **www.librarieswest.org.uk**
or contact your library.

Your Borrower number and PIN are required.

Bristol Libraries

1805840160

'This book provides clear and inspirational hope for anyone with a dyslexic child. Like many excellent books it is written from personal experience. I strongly recommend it.'
                                    – Sian Griffiths, Education Editor, **The Sunday Times**

'This book shines a light on 23 successful people with dyslexia and demonstrates that having dyslexia should not hold you back from achieving your potential. With the right support and an inner determination, success can be within reach. These personal stories, generously shared, should be inspiring for all who live with dyslexia.'
                                    – Kevin Geeson, Chief Executive at Dyslexia Action

'I would recommend this to people diagnosed with dyslexia and their families. One invaluable message is that perseverance and determination can help people achieve. Another is that talents in the dyslexia profile may be underrated at school but of tremendous importance to society afterwards. One interesting recurring theme was the importance of parents and the difference they could make in helping their children believe in themselves; more than one said "that costs nothing"'
                                    – Bernadette McLean, Principal of the Helen Arkell Dyslexia Centre, UK

'Shining through these highly personal accounts of difficult schooldays and the struggle for understanding is an overwhelming sense of optimism. Dyslexia has shaped these personal histories, but has not limited their ambition or ultimate success. For many, the role of parents is a central unifying feature, parents who believed their children could achieve, regardless of academic success, and who provided the confidence and encouragement they needed. This is a book for parents to buy for their young people, to read together and to find inspiration and encouragement, and it also provides a refreshing perspective for those working in education.'
                                    – Dr Teresa Regan CPsychol AFBPsS, Principal Educational Psychologist,
                                    Catalyst Psychology Community Interest Company

'In my experience every person with dyslexia has amazing potential waiting to be untapped. Sadly, this potential is often missed by our exam focussed education system. But once dyslexic people find their passion and talent they can achieve extraordinary things, as this wonderful collection of interviews demonstrates. I hope this book inspires young people, educators and parents to focus on what dyslexic people CAN do, not just what they can't.'

– Kate Griggs, Dyslexia Campaigner (Xtraordinary People) and Founder & CEO of Untap.it

Creative
SUCCESSFUL
DYSLEXIC

Creative
SUCCESSFUL
DYSLEXIC

23 HIGH ACHIEVERS SHARE THEIR STORIES

MARGARET ROOKE

FOREWORD BY
MOLLIE KING

Jessica Kingsley *Publishers*
London and Philadelphia

Typeset using dyslexia-friendly fonts.

Disclaimer: All the views in the book are the participants' own and not necessarily the views of Dyslexia Action.

First published in 2016
by Jessica Kingsley Publishers
73 Collier Street
London N1 9BE, UK
and
400 Market Street, Suite 400
Philadelphia, PA 19106, USA

www.jkp.com

Copyright © Margaret Rooke 2016
Foreword copyright © Mollie King 2016

The Author and Contributors assert their right, under the Copyright, Designs and Patents Act 1988, to be identified as the authors of the Work.

All rights reserved. No part of this publication may be reproduced in any material form (including photocopying or storing it in any medium by electronic means and whether or not transiently or incidentally to some other use of this publication) without the written permission of the copyright owner except in accordance with the provisions of the Copyright, Designs and Patents Act 1988 or under the terms of a licence issued by the Copyright Licensing Agency Ltd, Saffron House, 6–10 Kirby Street, London EC1N 8TS. Applications for the copyright owner's written permission to reproduce any part of this publication should be addressed to the publisher.

Warning: The doing of an unauthorised act in relation to a copyright work may result in both a civil claim for damages and criminal prosecution.

Library of Congress Cataloging in Publication Data
A CIP catalog record for this book is available from the Library of Congress

British Library Cataloguing in Publication Data
A CIP catalogue record for this book is available from the British Library

ISBN 978 1 84905 653 3
eISBN 978 1 78450 163 1

Printed and bound in Great Britain

To L and S
Love Mum

'Everybody is a genius. But if you judge a fish by its ability to climb a tree, it will live its whole life believing that it is stupid.'

Albert Einstein

Contents

Foreword

When your child is diagnosed with dyslexia, all sorts of things can run through your mind. You may feel embarrassed that they are different, relieved to know what it is that is making them struggle, and scared that they won't do as well at school or work as you'd hoped; their future may not be as bright as you'd imagined. Exactly the same worries can be felt by a child with dyslexia, too.

For me, at the age of 11, it was a relief to identify why reading had always been so difficult. The diagnosis gave my parents and my school important information about what I needed to help me progress.

Even now, dyslexia has an impact on my life. When The Saturdays are recording a new song for the first time, the other girls just 'go for it' and get going with the words. I have to study the lyrics quietly by myself for some time first. If I'm on TV, before I read a line from an autocue I have to memorise it first to make sure I don't make any mistakes.

When I think back to my school days, standing up in class and reading out loud, I remember my friend having to whisper words to me to help me through. I felt so puzzled when the others seemed to find their school work so much easier. I hated the amount of time it took me to make my way through my homework!

When I was reading the stories in this compilation it occurred to me that, while a lot more improvements are desperately needed in schools across the country, there is certainly a far greater awareness of dyslexia.

There are terrible stories from some of the older contributors of brutal treatment from teachers, of bullying and a general, shocking, ignorance about learning difficulties. Despite these harsh times, and feeling 'thick' and 'stupid', everyone in this book has fought their way through and achieved fantastically in their careers. They all talk about how dyslexia brought misery – but also how it helped them achieve. They may not have been top of the class, but there **is** life after school – and it was then that their creativity, determination and outlook helped them to get to where they wanted to be. Often there was at least one adult who was really on their side and helped them to move forwards.

People at school laughed when I said I wanted to be a singer as it was so different from what they were planning for themselves, but I knew I wanted this more than anything. I know that self-belief and confidence can be key to overcoming life's challenges and achieving our dreams, and the stories in this book underline that.

I hope you will read this book and feel inspired that dyslexia doesn't have to mean not doing as well as people whose minds work differently. There are great organisations that can help, including Dyslexia Action, which is receiving proceeds from the sales of this book.

Whether you are reading this book or having it read to you, I hope you will keep your confidence and ambition intact. Work as hard as you can – that's really important. See yourself for all your wonderful qualities and keep pushing to make your dreams come true. Mine have – and I hope yours will too.

Mollie King
The Saturdays
Ambassador, Dyslexia Action

Acknowledgements

Thank you to everyone who has been interviewed for this book, for your time, trust and insights. Thanks to Jessica Kingsley and the teams at Jessica Kingsley Publishers and Dyslexia Action (especially Becky Whitman and Emma Malcolm) for your help and enthusiasm. Thanks to my agent, Jane Judd, for all your encouragement and assistance. Additional thanks to Viv Fowle, Sarah Neville and Nicole Sochor for your skills and input, which I could not have done without, and also to Aggie MacKenzie, Eileen Maybin, Anne Metcalfe and Joanne Rule. Thank you to everyone who has been interested in this project for keeping me going, and special thanks and love, as ever, to Terry, Loretta and Shea.

Introduction

When our daughter was diagnosed with dyslexia at 13, we were shocked. She had seemed to steer herself through her early years of education without difficulty. In a world that seems obsessed with test results and exam grades, we had innocently presumed that whatever her struggles in life were going to be, they would not be academic.

But by 11 she had all but stopped learning and the realisation that something was not right, followed by a diagnosis of dyslexia, meant we suddenly had no idea of what the future might hold. The world of special needs, extra time in exams, slow processing speed and poor working memory was not what we had envisioned for her. In fact it took a couple of years for this all to sink in.

I talked about this to another mother I know. Katie remembers finding out her son was dyslexic at six. Unlike our daughter, Tom was at a competitive, highly academic school. One parents' evening, she saw a story he had written pinned to a classroom wall. Compared to the efforts of his classmates, it looked like the work of a much younger child.

'This was the first indication that something was wrong. Especially at a school like that, it was embarrassing,' Katie remembers. 'An educational psychologist diagnosed dyslexia and, although we were of course familiar with the term, we knew nothing about what this would mean for Tom. I remember feeling somehow our son was disabled.' Tom, in turn, was despondent.

That very week she spotted a story in a newspaper that mentioned that businessman Sir Richard Branson was dyslexic, along with many other leading entrepreneurs. She immediately cut out the article and stuck it to her son's bed. It is still there today, 14 years later.

From that moment, Tom started to gain hope. He was moved to a school that suited him better and he has just achieved, at 20, a first-class degree at a top London university. The family was delighted to hear that Sir Richard Branson's story is included here.

The idea for this book came from my own experience, Katie's experience, and the experiences of our children and of other families I have met in playgrounds and parents' meetings along the way. I knew a book like this would be of great encouragement for many. Its aim is to reassure anyone with dyslexia and their loved ones – together with any others who do not seem to shine naturally at school in these results-driven days.

This book can show them that, even though they may be struggling with their education now, or may have found school work difficult some decades ago, the future can be bright for them. A diagnosis of dyslexia is not something that has to condemn anyone to the scrapheap. Being top of the class at school is not the only way to achieve in life. There are many ways to succeed with dyslexia. Some people even regard it as an advantage, as all of the interviewees in this book attest.

Many giants of history are said to have had dyslexia, including Albert Einstein, Lewis Carroll, Leonardo da Vinci, Galileo Galilei and Agatha Christie. They have been joined in more recent times by Steven Spielberg, Muhammad Ali and Steve Jobs. No wonder that in their book, **The Dyslexic Advantage**,[1] Dr Brock L. Eide and Dr Fernette F. Eide describe dyslexia as a 'learning or processing style' with its own strengths and benefits, rather than a 'learning disorder'.

A recent study by Julie Logan of the CASS Business School and Nicola Martin of the London School of Economics[2] looks at successful entrepreneurs with dyslexia. It breaks new ground by providing evidence that the positive aspects of dyslexia can benefit organisations and individuals. It highlights that those with dyslexia can claim good spoken communication, good people skills, a great enthusiasm, often good sales ability

---

1   **The Dyslexic Advantage.** Hay House, London, 2011. Dr Brock L. Eide and Dr Fernette F. Eide.

2   'Unusual Talent: a Study of Successful Leadership and Delegation in Entrepreneurs who have Dyslexia.' **Journal of Inclusive Practice in Further and Higher Education.** Issue 4.1, October 2012, pp.57–76. Julie Logan and Nicola Martin.

thanks to an interest in others, and the capacity to delegate. In fact the authors say, 'The ability to delegate is an essential task if the business is to grow and we see this skill in many dyslexic entrepreneurs. This is because dyslexics often learn early in life to trust those around them to do the things they are not so good at.'

In addition, **The Sunday Times** newspaper has reported that the British intelligence agency recruits people with dyslexia in order to combat threats such as foreign espionage. It finds that while people with dyslexia may struggle with reading and writing they may excel at, for example, deciphering facts from patterns or events.[3]

From the interviews I have conducted for this book I have found that what united most (though not all) of those featured, from the poor to the privileged, is that they had a parent or teacher who encouraged them when they were young and gave them the sense that they were clever. Even though they may have felt stupid at school, they often had a confidence that came from an adult at home or another grown up who believed in them. This is something that all parents of children with dyslexia can give their children. Financially, it costs nothing. Emotionally, it can transform lives.

---

3   'Dyslexic Spies Sharpen GCHQ's Senses.' **The Sunday Times.**
     21 September 2014. Richard Kerbaj, Security Correspondent.

Dyslexia Action's Director of Education and Policy Dr John Rack confirms that the single most important response to a diagnosis of dyslexia is to be positive, even though it is a condition that affects fluent word reading and spelling, and can also have an impact on memory, organisation, mathematics and more.

Dr Rack says he often tells those he is assessing, 'I know that it's frustrating to have good ideas or to know the answer to a question and have difficulty writing it down. But think how much worse it would be if you were good at writing things down but didn't have any good ideas or didn't know any answers.'

He adds, 'Dyslexia can make people frustrated and lead them to doubt their abilities but, given what we know today, there is no reason for dyslexia to stop people from pursuing their goals and following their dreams.'

He stresses that it is not enough to tell children to believe in themselves, work harder and get over the problem. 'These things are easy to say but not easy to carry through. Learners of all ages need help and support. They need strategies and tricks to help them get better at what they find hard. They need people who can help them to have confidence when they doubt themselves. They need advice on how to get the best out of schools, colleges, night classes and any other places of learning. They need help from organisations including Dyslexia Action to help them on their way.'

And Dr Rack encourages adults to talk to children about the difficulties they may have faced at school. 'When children have dyslexia, it is almost always the case that there are others in the family who have similar difficulties. I see children's eyes widen when a mum or dad says, "I was the same at school. I could never spell very well…" The key for parents is to be understanding and positive and to look outwards for solutions to help them and their children to do the best they can.'

There is much more that schools can do to help pupils with dyslexia, and the stories of achievement within this book make a powerful case for the Government and education authorities to invest more to help all children to fulfil their potential.

Many in prison struggled at school and are unable to read and write. This suggests that other aspects of our society could be improved if more resources and attention were devoted to tackling problems with learning. Sir Jackie Stewart, whose story is featured in this book, is involved with inspirational work in Scotland to help prisoners with dyslexia find a new path. Children learn in so many different ways and expecting them all to acquire the same knowledge in the same way cannot possibly be the best way forward.

We all have different skills and attributes. Some of us are artistic, some are extremely caring, some can inspire. Others are great lorry drivers, chefs, builders, inventors or singers. Let's help our children and ourselves develop to our fullest potential – and celebrate what makes us all special.

I love mistakes. Mistakes send you somewhere
else. If something goes wrong I use that mistake,
I twist it around to make the most of what's
there. A lot of art is based on a mistake.

David Bailey CBE

World-renowned photographer, one of the most
influential of all time. In the 'silly class' at school
where he was caned for not being able to spell.
Hollywood films were his education – it was cheaper
to go to the cinema than feed the gas meter.

Dyslexia makes me see things differently. It makes my mind
work differently and I'm glad to have it.

I have a very intellectual friend who is one of the country's
best art critics. We decided to take a picture of the same view
in Cornwall. He had to agree that mine was much better and
had an atmosphere his lacked. I achieve this without being
able to explain why.

Maybe if I could understand it I wouldn't be able to do
it. It's just something that comes naturally and I put it down
to being dyslexic. It's the easiest thing in the world to be a
photographer, but turning a photograph into a creative work
of art is different. Someone can be taught photography and
have no passion and no soul. A musician can be unable to read

music and can be brilliant at what he does and the same can be true with photography.

When I make an image, I'm not interested in composition and rules. It's the emotion that is important. When I meet someone I notice things, I observe without judging, and how the picture turns out will depend on the person whose portrait I am making.

My wife Catherine says I have 'uncommon sense' in that I see things in people straight away. I look at the way they're dressed, their hair colour, eyes, glasses, jewellery and work them out. I see their body language and know who they are. It's instinctive and it can't be taught. It's just what I do.

I also believe film cameras have personalities. With digital you can see what you're photographing immediately so there is no mystery and no chance of mistakes. You stop taking photographs because you think you've got the shot you want. With film you never know when you've got it so you always go for something more.

I love mistakes. Mistakes send you somewhere else. If something goes wrong I use that mistake, I twist it around to make the most of what's there. A lot of art is based on a mistake. If you could think of a mistake in advance you would be the greatest artist in the world.

My biggest talent is being curious. I want to know how everything works, how people think, how people operate, what they do, what their sex life is like, what makes them happy, whether they're ambitious. Everyone is interesting, everyone's got a story and that all feeds into my work.

I have always had that curiosity. When I was young I remember making little museums. I'd find a box – once I even broke my parents' record player to use the old wooden speaker – and I'd put in things of interest and label them, sticking on the labels with bits of tape. Things like, 'pigeon feather found in Wanstead Park', 'broken blue egg shell…I suppose from a blackbird…found in such a place'. Anything that seemed a bit unusual really.

My dad didn't give a fig about my education, but my mum knew there was something wrong with me and sent me to a private school, for £7.50 a term. There they thought I was stupid and arrogant and they believed I could have done the work if I'd tried. The headmaster – Skelton, a horrible man – used to cane me for not being able to spell. He made me stand up in class and he would embarrass me because he thought I was getting the words wrong on purpose. No one thought about dyslexia in those days. I thought I was stupid. Skelton was talking about me to my mum once and said, 'Someone's got to dig the road.'

I was always interested in drawing. I remember winning a City and Guilds award at 13 for painting Bambi. Art was all I remember doing well and my mum would say, 'My Dave's going to be a commercial artist.'

At school I was in the 'silly class' and I remember thinking being top of the silly class was better than being bottom of the smart class. I was good at making up stories but I couldn't put them down on paper. The rest of the time I couldn't understand why they were teaching me things I wasn't interested in, like algebra. Even in the art lessons they'd tell me not to draw in outlines and I would think, 'Disney draws in outlines and I think he knows more than you.'

I understood Picasso's pictures as soon as I saw them. I knew he was magic. Seeing his pictures changed my life. I realised there were no rules. The school said I couldn't draw with an outline and Picasso did. So who's smarter, the teacher or Picasso?

The best thing about the school was that they didn't check up on you if you didn't go, so I used to go to Epping Forest on my bike. One term I counted up and I'd gone in to school for 33 days.

Instead of school, Hollywood cinema was my education. We would go to the pictures to keep warm because it was cheaper than feeding the gas meter and it took me to other worlds and made me think about other things. After I left school one of my friends called me a punk for not being able to read so I taught myself by learning what the words look like. This means I can read but I can't spell. I am 'word blind'. Sometimes I get even simple words wrong. I think I would have been fine with reading Chinese hieroglyphs which are so visual.

I went to the Boy Scouts just once. They showed us ten things on a table and then covered them over with a cloth and asked us to write down what they all were. I knew what they all were but I couldn't write any of them down. After that I was too embarrassed to stay and I never went back.

After I left school I did various jobs and was then drafted into the air force for my National Service. When I did tests there, again I knew all the answers but didn't know how to write them down. I still wouldn't be able to do this. In the air force they saw the images I was taking and suggested that I go to the London School of Printing and Graphic Art to study photography but when I applied they wouldn't let me in because they said I needed a maths and English GCE. I didn't even know what a GCE was and, anyway, what had that got to do with photography?

I'd been interested in photography since I was 12 and started messing around with my mum's old box Brownie. I'd started off photographing birds because I loved birds and wanted to be an ornithologist until I found out this would mean learning the Latin names and I hadn't managed to learn English yet.

After the air force I became an assistant to the photographer John French. My first published portrait was of Somerset Maugham for **Today** magazine in 1960. Soon after I began working at **Vogue**.

Although I was successful I found my word blindness embarrassing. When I was with one of my first girlfriends, Jean Shrimpton, she sent me out to buy a couple of doormats. I came back with five or six. She asked me why I had bought that many and I said I had to get to a price I could spell on the cheque. My world changed when the credit card was invented and I didn't have to worry about spelling.

This word 'dyslexia' appeared when I was about 30. I would read things about it and hear people talking about it. It made sense as to why my girlfriends would say to me, 'You're a bit absent minded, you're not listening, that's not what I was talking about.' Catherine still finds this with me.

I often think people understand what I am saying when they don't. I say something and it makes me think about something else by association. I can't read eight pages without being distracted and thinking about something else. I get bored easily. I can't concentrate. Sometimes I have to write things for the books I bring out and half a page takes me a couple of hours. Catherine can read what I write despite my spelling but after a couple of days I forget what it is about. She can read it better than me. She's more patient than me.

I have directed at least 500 commercials (for the NSPCC, Greenpeace and other charities). As soon as I get the script I can see what the film would look like from beginning to end. To me it's all common sense. But it's difficult to get the message out there about dyslexia. You can feature a child with flies on his face or a child in a wheelchair but dyslexia is not emotive enough for politicians. They are missing an opportunity – dyslexics are smart. We think differently. Catherine always says by not supporting people with dyslexia properly the country is losing a generation of different thinkers.

We have three children and they are all dyslexic and we told them just to do their best in school. The education system is something they had to get through. What is important for children is to find out what they are good at and incorporate it into what they need to learn.

I think it's probably good that my kids are dyslexic. After all, if dyslexics wrote the IQ tests the smart-arses wouldn't pass. It all depends who's setting the tests. I believe if you have curiosity and spark you will do well. That's why there are so many dyslexic photographers, artists and filmmakers.

We are all different and we need to come together to make society work. What would happen if everyone was a scientist? We need the musicians. If I was in a trench in the First World War and they were coming over the hill to get me I wouldn't want an academic next to me. I would want a dyslexic – or a gangster like Ron Kray. It would be, 'All right Ron, we can deal with this.' We are not going to think like the rest. Together we will think of a way to get round them or distract them or tell a joke and make them laugh. Or punch them and run…!

When you are dyslexic you are often told…'You're a failure. You won't be able to do it,' while I had been brought up being told, 'You can do it. You can, you can…' Maybe this is why when someone tells me I can't do something, I find I want it all the more.

Ed Baines

TV chef, restaurateur, author and owner of Randall & Aubin in central London. One school was a mystery to him, the next a war zone. Finally he found a school to give him confidence.

When I was 12 years old I decided school was not necessary. The place was a catastrophe; I really couldn't see the point of it all.

I found lots of ways of pretending I was going to school. I spent a lot of time on London Underground, visiting almost every station on the map. I would also go off and visit places: Camden Market; the Natural History, Science, and Victoria and Albert Museums. I spent time there instead.

The school was an inner London state school: rough and run-down. It supposedly had remedial facilities so I was taken out of my class for extra English lessons for two hours a week on Tuesday and Thursday afternoons. The other children noticed this and of course the bullying started. I definitely wasn't going to allow that, so in retaliation I stood my ground.

I wanted to hold my position in the pecking order and I got into a fair old bit of trouble. This school, for me, became a war zone.

I grew up in Chiswick, west London. Together with my older brothers, I had been going to Bedford Park Preparatory School to help me get into a selective independent school such as Latymer or St Paul's.

My two elder brothers were at Latymer and I went and sat the exams and got into Latymer prep, the junior school. It can be very difficult to identify dyslexia early on and if you're intelligent and articulate you can deal with a lot of exam questions, and three-dimensional puzzles and problem-solving codes are all straightforward.

I look back now and realise that once I was there I really didn't know what I was doing. I remember thinking, 'I don't know what's going on – I wonder if anyone else does.'

In my second year it was a bit like the Charlie Brown cartoon scenario, when the teacher just seems to be making a droning noise and you're not really getting any of it. I was slightly oblivious to it all and copied work from the person sitting next to me. I really enjoyed being there and wasn't even aware of being different. Then the headmaster said to my mother, 'We think Edward has learning difficulties. He's not going to be able to go to the upper school.'

In a school like that they don't have additional facilities to give you extra support. You either cut the grade or you're out.

My mother took me to see a specialist and she immediately recognised I was dyslexic. I was knocked by it. There is always a rivalry between brothers and their academic journey was certainly smoother.

I ended up at the inner city school but I was very good at intercepting all the correspondence between the school and my mother. Then one of the letters slipped past my 'system'. They asked my mum to attend a parents' evening and told her, 'We don't really see much of Edward. We don't know where he is.'

It was the first Mum knew that I hadn't been turning up. My mother was widowed when we were children so she had to keep us afloat and worked extremely hard. I generally bottled everything up and dealt with it by myself. Fortunately she had the ability to talk to me about how I felt in a calm and accepting way, without making it into a big deal. We had a heart-to-heart and decided we should look at other schools.

I was very fortunate to end up at Stanbridge, a boarding school, but my mother had to work extremely hard to afford it. At this school there were just 280 of us and I made lifelong friends. It changed me and my life.

Nearly all of us had been naughty in other schools. When you're not with the herd as a child, one tends to rebel: you get frustrated, disenfranchised, angry. But at Stanbridge we all had something in common.

Dyslexia isn't a gauge for intelligence. Some people with dyslexia are bright, some are not. But if you are dyslexic you are riddled with frustration because an awful lot of things you get very quickly, and then you come across this wall of things you don't understand. Also dyslexic people tend to think in a structured kind of way, which can lead to success, but there are tendencies to be stubborn when getting stuck. Our attitude tends to be, 'This is how things **should** be.'

Stanbridge gave me a big advantage. I remember becoming confident. You tend to be defensive about dyslexia when you are in the minority, but when everyone's dyslexic it's no longer an issue. It becomes a case of, 'You drive on the left; I drive on the right.'

The school focused on what we were good at. We concentrated as well on the creative side of education and also on sporting achievements. We had to do the five staples: maths, English, biology, chemistry and physics, but then we'd have motor mechanics, drama, art, design, pottery… They managed to find an awful lot of alternative subjects to study.

Depending on how dyslexic you were, there was also intense, additional, one-to-one tuition with a remedial teacher. I had eight hours a week with Mrs Drysdale. I automatically wrote in a dyslexic way, as words sound, but this was drummed out of me. This meant I was at last able to read and write properly-ish. I now use spellcheck which is a great tool, although sometimes my spelling is so far off the mark I have to put the word into Google. Just yesterday, I was writing some recipes and wrote 'de-sinew the lamb fillets' but I couldn't work out how to spell sinew.

I wasn't interested in cooking when I was at school, though I loved eating. Later, when I looked back on my childhood, all I remembered was the food. My mother is an adventurous cook and I remember sitting in the pushchair as a child, going round the delis, butchers and greengrocers with her.

I didn't know what I was going to do with my working life. If you're dyslexic, it can be a struggle to join the traditional professions, though a couple of my school friends are in finance, and they are very good at it. The majority have taken an alternative route and they are more comfortable there. A lot of families send their children to prep schools, selective schools, university, and the city. It's mapped out for them from the age of five onwards. If you're dyslexic you might have to look at life in a slightly wider way.

When I left school I was at home not doing much, driving my mother mad. Eventually I was instructed to go out and get a job and stay out until I had one. An older friend of my brothers worked as a chef in the Dorchester Hotel. I went there for a job interview, was accepted there and I loved it. I was given an apprenticeship and worked under Anton Mosimann. I loved the regimental, structured nature of the work. There was a lot of responsibility and the expectation to show up and do your job well.

I had no real long-term plan and no structure or ambition, but every week I got paid and I learned new things. It was tough but I enjoyed it.

The same friend then went on to work for Wind Star sail cruises, beautiful cruise yachts. He contacted me and said, 'You'll love this.' So I went off to sea. I worked on board seven days a week for six months, 15 hours a day. It was a bit like training for the Olympics but in haute cuisine. It was tough but good.

On board, I worked alongside a German chef whose nickname for me was 'English'. He'd often say, 'English, you won't make it.' When you are dyslexic you are often told at points of childhood, 'You're a failure. You won't be able to do it,' while I had been brought up being told, 'You can do it. You can, you can, you can.' Maybe this is why when someone tells me I can't do something, I find I want it all the more.

So this man's attitude made me determined to keep at it for the six months, as painful as it was. This was to be the backbone of my career as the work we did there was so advanced. After this, cooking was plain sailing. I went to Australia and cooked there for two years and realised my ambition was to own a restaurant in London. When I opened Randall & Aubin in London's Soho, I thought, 'I've cracked it.'

If you're dyslexic and receive encouragement, the dyslexia can be a driving force. You can be a bit 'chippy', which can give you a determination to succeed and never give up. Wanting to prove people wrong who've written you off can be a real motivator! I was called stupid quite regularly as a young boy so I really wanted to do well.

When I became successful I would go to the pub a lot when I was stressed or angry, dealing with my frustrations in the wrong way. Success didn't feel like I'd thought it would feel. I had achieved something I'd worked very, very hard for. For periods of my life nothing else had mattered except achieving and being successful. I had become incredibly driven, selfish and antisocial because I was so focused on wanting to achieve. Then, when I had become successful, it wasn't what I thought it was going to be. I wasn't happy. I hadn't found the right balance.

If I had continued down that road I think I would have ended up in prison because I'd become self-destructive. The saving grace for me was boxing, the gym and the swimming pool. They rebalanced me. Exercise was a release. I found there was something very cleansing about training hard and swimming. It cleared my system.

The relentless ambitious drive has gone. Randall & Aubin, which I co-own in central London, is an intimate and environmentally conscious restaurant, which is much smaller than people expect but it is just the way we want it to be. My drive is no longer based on proving anything. It's just to work hard and be the best at what we do.

Sometimes I have thought being dyslexic is an advantage, but I also think things are harder without a doubt. You need to put more effort in.

When I write books I have to hand over what I've written for someone to sort out and read again and make changes. Then I read it again to make sure they haven't eliminated personality from it.

For me, the often unsung real heroes of the foundation of the British restaurant revolution are Alistair Little, Simon Hopkinson, Rowley Leigh, Rose Gray and certainly Marco Pierre White and Raymond Blanc – I like intelligent, academic cooks who write in detail. And always the training on board the yacht has never really left me although I cook in a far more natural way, and I learned this from Rose and Ruth at the River Cafe.

Jamie Oliver's cooking is what I would call dyslexic. He has an incredibly flamboyant, fearless approach. His natural side is all there without the academic French techniques. He does some bonkers things. It's simple and it works.

There are always challenges when you are dyslexic, but I had an injection of confidence as a child from my mother. She didn't say everything was fantastic. If something's crap, it is crap. She saw my mind from a creative side. She saw what I was focusing on and helped me.

As a parent you don't want to overdo the pressure because children will rebel. A few hours a week of extra learning is enough. Parents may not be best placed to do this teaching. Children want to look confident in front of their parents, not descend into a spiral of shame.

But there are lots of ways in which parents can help. For instance, I know someone whose son is dyslexic and the moment they put a yellow piece of Perspex over the page the letters stopped moving.

I say, try not to make big hoo-ha about dyslexia because the child will think there's something wrong with them. There's nothing wrong with them. Their brain works differently – some might say more efficiently. It's as simple as that.

We have to keep finding new, innovative ways to live our lives. The dyslexic people I know are brilliant in how they think in different ways. It is a gift, a great thing to have.

Charley Boorman

TV motorcycle adventurer, President of Dyslexia Action. Battled with his teachers as he tried to explain dyslexia to them.

My dad is the film director John Boorman and when I was six or seven we were travelling all over America as he was shooting **Deliverance**. Because of that we had lots of tutors and luckily one of them picked up that I was dyslexic – she had just learned about the condition. In the US they were streets ahead of us in the UK. They had machines for kids to play with to help us learn to read and write and all sorts of other gadgets that I didn't see on this side of the world for years.

What was tricky was that the rest of the time we were living in Ireland where they didn't seem to have a clue about dyslexia and what it was. I felt very frustrated as I kept having to explain to my teachers what it meant. They would say, 'Boorman, stand up and read,' and I would say, 'I can't, I'm dyslexic.' Some of the teachers thought I was taking the piss and didn't understand. It was a bit of a battle with them. I knew what I had, but they didn't.

I would get into terrible trouble and sent to the headmaster and told to stop mucking around. In fact I did do a lot of mucking around and I know a lot of kids who are dyslexic do become the class clown to distract from their weaknesses or to get attention they're not getting in other ways.

School life was tough. I was terrible at learning because I wasn't able to read and when people say you are stupid you do believe them. I was being earmarked as being thick and pushed to the side. I was definitely given the impression that I would not amount to much.

While the messages I was getting from school were very damaging, my parents never made me feel anything other than a confident little boy. My father had spotted the signs of dyslexia too and he encouraged me to be in the films he made as a way to express myself because I couldn't read or write properly. Dad felt that if I acted it would help me be surer of myself. I did bits and pieces for him, appearing in scenes, and I started to enjoy it and learn that I could communicate through acting.

If you are lucky enough to have the support of your family, life is so much better. If you get a diagnosis as well you have the chance to get the tools to help you on your way. You need these tools because you can't get fixed. There is no fix.

For me, it was a relief to know what I had. I knew I had problems with my short-term memory and trouble with this and that and suddenly I realised I was not alone with it. Because of my early dyslexia diagnosis I was taught ways of helping myself which I still use.

Dad spent a lot of time with me when I was young. We would sit and learn together every day. There's a lovely bit in the book about his life where he talks about this. When I was very small I also had a terrible stutter and I really did struggle to express myself, but I was helped by all the hard work from Dad.

I remember when he was teaching me he would give me one word to read, one simple word. The next day I would have forgotten it. He would say, 'For God's sake,' because it is frustrating but he was incredibly patient and it does take time and a huge amount of patience. I found it very difficult to retain anything in my head but the more acting I did and the more lines I learned pushed my boundaries. I just kept repeating, repeating, repeating. I always knew I had other strengths and these were especially helped by the acting, which gave me something to focus on. It's a bit like when someone has lost an eye and their other senses seem to get sharper.

Then I went to a Quaker school near Banbury which had a great dyslexic centre. I was always being taken out of class to do English, maths and history for 'special lessons'. It was hard work but that's just the way it was. Because there were other kids with dyslexia there, I didn't feel so alienated.

I got four O-levels, though not at good grades, and then I got a part in a movie so I left. I was very lucky that I knew what I wanted to do which was to be an actor and I'd already had some experience. Scripts were a nightmare though so I had to learn them in segments, a few sentences at a time.

When you're dyslexic it can feel as if it's a privilege because you're forced to see the world in a different way and think differently at school and at work. You have to do this to survive. A dyslexic person can also be much more visual than someone who isn't. For me, learning is all about the visuals, not enormous words.

I was quite successful in the 80s, and then my acting career faded out. I think it was partly because I kept choosing movies based on the location, rather than the script. I would be sitting on a plane going to Africa, reading the script, thinking, 'Oh dear…'

Then I met Ewan McGregor when we were filming **The Serpent's Kiss** and we found we had a joint love of motorbikes. We filmed **Long Way Round** and **Long Way Down**, BMW motorcycle trips across the world, and now people see me as an adventurer, not an actor.

I think one of the things my adventuring has taught me is that I am a good businessman. All the TV shows I have done are made by a production company I help run. We think up the ideas, raise the money and do the whole thing. There is a whole raft of other entrepreneurial people who are dyslexic, who are creative because of the way they think. We have to keep finding new, innovative ways to live our lives. The dyslexic people I know are brilliant in how they think in different ways. It is a gift, a great thing to have.

A lot of my time now is spent taking people on adventure trips across Africa from Cape Town to the Victoria Falls on BMW motorbikes. I was born into a family that travelled all over the world to make movies and because of this, a sense of adventure is in me.

I am President of Dyslexia Action and one of our jobs is to try to get people to realise that it is a debilitating thing to have, though with the right education and tools you can live with it very easily.

People who have disabilities – visual, hearing or wherever else – can very often excel in other ways and it's a matter of finding those ways.

If you're confident about being dyslexic, people are quite happy to accommodate you when you tell them. There isn't so much stigma about it, though some still think you are making it up, or you're thick. I always think it's important to know your weaknesses and delegate when you can't do something. I haven't been able to help my kids with their homework since they were seven.

I would like to see the Government have someone in every school who is able to identify that a kid has dyslexia at a young age and help them. This is one of the big things Dyslexia Action wants to achieve.

I say to children it doesn't matter what the other kids can do, it matters what you can do. Find your strengths and work on these. Going to university is not the be-all and end-all in life. It's a very small part of it and you don't have to go. Modern technology brings with it so many different opportunities; nothing should hold you back.

Parents can play a huge part in helping. They are always the ones in the background pushing their children on. It's hugely important for parents to know where to go for help. If you're lucky you will find your way to Dyslexia Action or a school that will support you.

I come across kids who break my heart and I see a lot of myself in them. Dyslexia can be so frustrating for children. It can be frustrating for teachers too to spend ages teaching a word to someone and the next day they still can't spell it. But it's really great when kids come into Dyslexia Action and they get assessed and asked, 'Do you find this or that difficult?' and their eyes light up and they realise they are not alone and that all the things that have irked or frustrated them and their parents…they find out it's okay and it's normal. That's what I love to see.

I've also visited a project in Nottingham run with probation officers that aims to help reduce rates of reoffending by improving the levels of illiteracy among the offenders. One main goal here is to help them find work.

Some people do slip through the net and are so crippled by dyslexia that they don't know what to do. They can withdraw into themselves. Everyone should have the opportunity to gain the tools to get them through.

Times can be hard and there are obstacles to climb but with help and support you can achieve what you want in life.

Accept you are different, question what others don't, trust
your instincts, go for the opportunities others miss…

Sir Richard Branson

The Virgin Group founder says of school, 'The blackboard was all a-jumble.' He left at 15 to start creating one of the world's most recognised brands.

In business, I believe dyslexia is my greatest strength. It has taught me to keep things simple, to rise above difficulties and to focus on what I'm good at, while delegating the rest. Dyslexia has forced me to uncover my own strengths by trying out different approaches. I have had to build on my different ways of thinking to establish and maintain the success of the Virgin Group of companies.

In fact I have met many dyslexics in my lifetime who have excelled because they weren't great at the conventional way of doing things. They have taken an unconventional approach to life and succeeded.

Everyone makes mistakes and this is certainly the case in the world of business. Dyslexia has helped teach me not to be embarrassed by my failures. I have always learnt from them and started again. I've said before that children don't learn to walk by following rules. They learn by trying, falling down and doing it again. It's that simple.

At school being dyslexic meant I couldn't follow what was being taught in lessons so I became distracted. In business I've realised that it's still the case that if I'm not interested in something I don't take in what's being said. This means that if I do grasp an idea I know it is something that is easily understood, clear and straightforward. When I'm at work it is always one of my priorities to simplify messages and ideas that are complex and not easy to understand. I think this is one of the reasons that we are one of the world's most recognised and successful brands.

Virgin is Europe's most diversified group of private companies. We operate in many different sectors including travel, mobile phones, financial services and health. Now we are going into space. If I am starting up a new venture, I don't spend a long time researching the finances and working out all the figures in advance to show how it might perform. Details can be important but it's more important for me not to get bogged down by them. I look for the patterns and the bigger picture.

I often go with my gut feelings and instinct and then delegate the work to someone who can do it better than me. I've had to learn to trust others with tasks and stop trying to do things myself, including some reading and writing. Delegation is a skill some people don't develop but if you're dyslexic you have to. I go ahead with an idea and hope we will create something special that makes a difference to other people's lives and that the figures will add up at the end of the year. But I always get someone else to do the sums!

It's been a priority for me to recruit people who are better than me and it's my job to inspire them, to help draw out the best from them. My focus is on creative thinking and building strategies for new ventures – which is what I am good at – and they focus on making the other ventures work successfully.

Einstein, who I understand was dyslexic, has been quoted as saying that it's a miracle that curiosity survives a formal education. I wasn't academically successful and this hasn't stopped me being successful outside of school. If you have dyslexia it is important to accept that you are different. I knew at a very young age that I needed to get out of school and make my own way in life.

I don't even know whether the word dyslexia had been invented when I was a child. It was generally decided at school that I was a hopeless case. I remember sitting at the back of the class and not knowing what was going on. The blackboard was all a-jumble. I once had an IQ test where I sat looking at the paper and getting nowhere.

Even though my schoolwork was poor, I didn't ever think I was stupid. Luckily for me I came from a wonderful family and had lots of love from them. They just wanted the best for me, though they were obviously slightly worried about my exam results and my future. The one good thing for me at school was that I excelled at games and was captain of the football and cricket teams. Then I had an injury that stopped me playing.

If I had carried on excelling at games I almost definitely would have stayed on at school, so out of this adversity came a new opportunity and approach to life.

I remember walking around the garden with my dad at 15 and saying to him, 'I'm thinking of leaving school.' We went around the garden many times deep in conversation and in the end he said, 'You know what you want to do with your life and you're 15. I didn't know what I wanted to do when I was 21. So leave school, give it a go and if it doesn't work out we will try to get you an education.'

I found out later on in life what he was actually thinking, 'He's a hopeless case at school and anything's better than him carrying on getting nowhere there.'

Bizarrely I had started plotting a magazine – of all things to do for someone who's dyslexic – to give students a voice to speak out on school and global issues such as the war in Vietnam and I left school at 15 to make this work. So, to write for the magazine despite my dyslexia, I would interview people who spoke well and then transcribe it word for word rather than embellishing with my own thoughts.

I was fortunate to feature huge names of the time, such as the American novelist James Baldwin, the broadcaster Malcolm Muggeridge, the actor and political activist Vanessa Redgrave, and the philosopher Jean-Paul Sartre. I was quite cheeky. I got away with asking people for interviews because my voice had just broken. I was young and enthusiastic and I was a man with a cause so people were willing to give me time.

I was in my twenties when I suddenly heard about dyslexia. It was a bit of a relief. I had been taught that if you're no good in IQ tests you are hopeless. It was good to know that there was an issue and that other people had similar problems – and that actually dyslexics can be much brighter than other kids in certain areas. So it was a light-bulb moment and I grabbed it.

I am never quite sure if some of my characteristics are because of dyslexia or not. There are words I muddle up. I never know if the phrase is 'faux pas' or 'pas faux'. Often I find a lovely jumble of words coming out of my mouth and hopefully that makes people laugh. I think I have taught myself to get much better at speaking in public over the years after my tons of experience. I remember the very first interview I gave on the BBC to the journalist Anthony Howard. He cut out all my 'umms' and 'aahs' and told me the tape of my 'umms' and 'aahs' was longer than what was left.

I am learning all the time. When I turned 50 I was in a board meeting and by then we were the biggest private group of companies in Europe and Virgin was very well-known internationally. I was given some figures and I said, 'Is that good?' and one of the directors took me outside of the boardroom and said, 'Can I have a quiet word with you? You don't know the difference between "net" and "gross" do you?' I told him I didn't. He pulled out some paper, coloured in the sea blue, drew a fishing net in the sea, drew some fish in the net and said, 'In the net, that's your profit. That's what you've got left at the end of the year. That's what's yours.

The rest is turnover,' and from then on I've been namedropping 'net' and 'gross' all over the place.

It has been a strength of the Virgin culture and the Virgin company that I don't impose my ideas on people and I'm a good listener. Again this is because I know I'm by no means perfect and I think dyslexia plays a part in that. A lot of the instincts I developed from having dyslexia can apply to non-dyslexics as well. People ought to learn the art of delegation. They often don't do this because think they know everything. Learning to be a better listener is vital for everyone and maybe especially for someone running a company.

In schools I'm sure there really does need to be much more one-on-one, or two-on-one, teaching for people who are dyslexic. Extra time in exams is a step in the right direction – they definitely didn't have anything like that in my day.

The important thing for people who have learning difficulties is to push yourself and try to overcome anything holding you back. I believe most people can do this, though some will struggle more than others. When I was young my memory wasn't good and I've had to force it to get better. My spelling is sometimes still poor but I have managed to overcome the worst of my difficulties through training myself to concentrate.

If you can't overcome your difficulties, remember to try to focus on the things you enjoy. This will help build your confidence and give you more time for those things because you will leave behind the things you're not good at, to an extent. Be a people person, surround yourself with great people and draw on other people to compensate for your weaknesses.

Dyslexia has taught me to rise to challenges. Remember, if you are not exceptional academically you can still be exceptional. Accept you are different, question what others don't, trust your instincts, go for the opportunities others miss, keep an open mind and learn by what you do. If you follow your dreams, you can be even more successful than the others.

Because I struggled at school, being successful
feels like a victory. At the same time, it's not a
victory over dyslexia because dyslexia has given
me my particular way of looking at the world.

Marcus Brigstocke

Comedian and actor; well-known stand-up and regular on BBC Radio 4. Was fearful of reading and writing at school but his dyslexia was spotted early. He developed a love of books and has written his own.

I have a theory – which I certainly can't back up with any research – that a staggering number of comedians are dyslexic. I've seen their notebooks…

If school has been a challenge and you are behind or need extra help and if you are dyslexic, you may have your own way of looking at the world that might prepare you quite well for observing it in the way that comedians do.

Or it could be that you are reacting to failing to keep up with other people in the classroom and realise you get a reaction by making other people laugh.

Maybe it's the way that people with dyslexia use language. I think that dyslexia makes me a better comedian. On a very mechanical note, the way that I learned to read meant I broke down the words into their component parts, which means I see the construction of words – and that is helpful in writing comedy. It helps with spotting puns, it's helpful in the way I use language.

It may be that dyslexia itself is indicative of your brain working in a different way. I think dyslexia does make you look at the world slightly differently and that's worked well for me. It's hard to define how it makes you see the world differently but I do think that dyslexia is probably a little more complicated than struggling with words and language. It is a larger thing, which helps people become creative.

One mistake people make is thinking that if you're dyslexic it means you're slow. Extra time in exams has nothing to do with your brain working slowly. Even if the words you are reading or writing are coming out slowly, your brain is probably whizzing away at the same speed – or faster – than everybody else's. If anything, the problem I have in writing is that I can never get my hand moving quickly enough to get stuff down at the speed I'm thinking of it. It is frustrating if you have a story to tell.

I understand the challenge for teachers but if you've tuned out of a lesson and you're exploring your own imagination, this might help you become a great creative writer. There's also nothing more dispiriting than creating a story and it coming back covered in red ink because it is illegible and the spelling is terrible.

My handwriting was an illegible scrawl then and it still is, but it doesn't matter. I have written a book. Writing a book was difficult, but not because I am dyslexic. It was tough because it was lonely and challenging, and there was too much to hold in my head all at once. I typed it and thank God for spellcheck.

Writing a book was a big thing for me, a huge challenge. There's a little bit of me saying to myself, 'I make my living from reading and writing: I write stuff and then I read it out.' That's quite remarkable for someone for whom writing something down held a lot of fear, reading held a lot of fear, and making sense of words held a lot of fear. And now that's my stock in trade and I'm really good at it too.

At school I did feel different from the other kids and I suppose that's partly why I see the world differently. But I was lucky that my dyslexia was spotted very early on. My mum was a teacher so I had help from a very early age. When I was five or six, she observed me struggling with books and words, language and writing and then also having difficulty with concentration and focus. She sent me to be assessed and I got extra one-on-one teaching from when I was seven or eight. In a classroom you can disappear if you feel you have been left behind but if you're sitting there with Mrs Newby, as I was, she could spot when I wasn't concentrating.

As a kid dyslexia is one of those things that makes you think, 'There's something wrong with me, I wish I wasn't different, blah blah blah,' but it was never really a big, uncomfortable problem for me.

I probably was teased, but not hugely. I think teasing at school tends to be more about how you look or something weird you've done rather than not achieving academically. The much bigger issue I think is the demands that dyslexia places on teachers. When kids are staring out of the window, it's not because the teachers are bad, it's that how they are teaching won't work for all the kids. I need a lot of attention so I suppose I felt inadequate around my teachers. They were hard on me because I was a pain, not because I was dyslexic.

By the time I reached the age of 11, I found reading pleasurable. By the age of 13 I was reading on my own, unprompted. This was a sea change as it had been a challenge to read anything up until then. When I learned to read it became a passion and once I 'got' books and words they really became the most enormous pleasure.

At school I wasn't motivated at all. Yes, I was motivated by my own pleasure in reading, but I didn't read to improve myself academically. I just enjoyed the stories. Dyslexia can stop you enjoying stories because of the problems it brings with reading but it is worth persevering because stories are worth the effort.

If you're struggling to read, get audio books and read along with them. It takes the pressure off. If you're reading along and someone is saying what you're looking at, I think the two things will connect up in your brain.

Don't ever let dyslexia steal from you the joy that is storytelling because telling a story is one of the greatest things that humanity is able to do. Books are such an excellent and intimate way of doing this.

It's hard to say if dyslexia still hinders me. I can still sometimes find it difficult to concentrate while I'm reading. My mind attaches to ideas and spirals off quite easily. It's similar to what happened when I was really struggling when I was young and my mind would disappear off elsewhere.

I very often find when I'm reading books that I have to go back and read several pages again but I don't mind. I used to believe if I isolated myself I would be able to focus better but it makes absolutely no difference. I can immerse myself in a book in a crowded room with noisy people and music, and I can immerse myself in a book in an armchair.

When I'm acting I don't have a problem learning a script. I remember when I was in **Love Actually** and **The Railway Children** learning the lines in the rehearsal rooms. Once we have run through a scene twice I will have learned it. If I just had the script I would struggle with that, but when I can attach it to the actions and see the other actors and the scenery I learn it very quickly.

I don't think I was motivated to achieve until I was in my twenties. Being dyslexic hasn't made me more motivated but it has taught me not to overreact to dyslexia.

If you have children with dyslexia I would say, 'Just love them.' That's all that matters. Everything else will come to them and they will be all right. It may be that they will never be any good at reading and writing and that will probably mess up their education but if they are loved they will still be the people you want them to be. And always share stories with them. If books hold fear for them, continue to read to them. My son is 13 and he comfortably reads a chapter book a day but I still read to him and my daughter: not because they can't read themselves but because stories are the great connector. They bind people together. They fill the world with colour, light and laughter and make us able to understand other people's experiences – all of those wonderful things that are the point of being a person.

Because I struggled at school, being successful feels like a victory. At the same time, it's not a victory over dyslexia because dyslexia has given me my particular way of looking at the world.

If your child is diagnosed as dyslexic, don't imagine that that's a problem. It's just a difference. You will have to do a few

For me, in my life, dyslexia has been a little bit of a blessing. It helped me find my strength and directed me towards what I really wanted to do.

things differently and there are things to get o
all be fine. If reading and writing are a problem
more than be making up for it in other ways. Tl
great artists, they might be able to sing, they m
they might well be sporty. I think dyslexia is ov
in comedy but just take a look in the sporting

Darcey Bussell CBE

Once one of the great British ballerinas, now a TV favourite as a judge on **Strictly Come Dancing.** She used to hide in a cupboard at school to avoid classes.

Hiding in a cupboard was my way of avoiding the relentless struggle of lessons at primary school. I can still remember nestling among the exercise books and pencils with the teacher knocking on the door pleading, 'Come on, Darcey. Come down to class.'

My primary school in west London was meant to be quite open to the idea of dyslexia and other learning conditions, but for many years the teachers thought I was being lazy. Then they realised that, when it came to subjects I thought I could handle, I worked very hard. My problem was when the lesson was on a subject I found difficult, such as reading or writing or maths. Then I would do anything to try to escape from it. Which is why, from when I was about eight, I would sneak into the cupboard and hope no one would spot me.

I had other ways of avoiding tasks that felt impossible to deal with. If we were asked to write a story about something and illustrate it with a picture, the writing part was the most horrible challenge for me. So I would work on the illustration for an hour and a half and then write three lines for the story, making sure there was 'no time' to finish it.

When I was eight we went to live in Australia for a short while, and I did a term at a school in Sydney. It was there that this realisation hit me. I compared my reading book to those of the other children and saw I was reading books for younger children.

Back in the UK I tried to catch up, constantly trying to reach the level of the others. I would pretend that they hadn't noticed my difficulties, telling myself, 'They don't really know how bad I am.'

One old-fashioned class teacher had a grading system and I was on the bottom table. Everybody travelled up the tables as they progressed and I never did, which was the most humiliating thing. He made us stand on our chairs and recite our times tables and we weren't allowed to get down until we had done them correctly. I was on that chair for a long time. He probably did it thinking I would improve but I knew I was always going to struggle.

Luckily I only had this teacher for one year. All the other teachers were fabulous and I felt fortunate that I was at a school where they didn't keep talking about who was at what level.

My mother always encouraged me by telling me everyone had different strengths – and it was true. I was arty and sporty.

I loved gymnastics and was even in the boys' football team. I was a child with a lot of energy and even sitting still was difficult. The teachers must have been exasperated with me. I must have been a nightmare to have in a classroom, totally exhausting. I was desperately waiting for the next distraction.

I did want to impress them, though. I loved history and worked hard at it but when we had tests I knew I would fail because of my spelling. I was never going to get the marks someone else would.

My good friends at school didn't bring up my difficulties and I would keep away from others who were cruel. I was bullied about being behind but, looking back, I don't see this as a negative. Of course it was tough at the time, but if I hadn't gone through that I wouldn't have gained the strength to grit my teeth and get on with things. There are some children who can't react like this, I know, but if you are being told at home, 'You're fine. Success will happen at a different time for you,' and are encouraged in the way I was by my parents then you do develop an ability to cope.

The diagnosis of dyslexia didn't come until secondary school at 11. When I was told, I felt I would have been better off not knowing. My mother had always made me believe that if I really wanted to achieve I could do it just with hard work, so I always thought I would improve. The terminology confirmed that my differences were part of me and the diagnosis lay heavily on my shoulders.

I went to extra classes for people with dyslexia at St Bartholomew's Hospital. Here I found out that I was turning words around the wrong way as I read them and wrote them. When I understood this I could help myself correct them. I also learned to revise by taping myself speaking about the subject and then listening to it back. A great idea!

I realised that whole pages of words overwhelmed me and I was taught to put a piece of card over the rest of the page while I read a line, which was a big help.

At school, which was a stage school, I had to memorise poems and I managed this. I had learned by now that if I wanted something enough I had to believe it was possible and fight to achieve it. I remember one teacher saying to me that I had the right physique to be a decent dancer and I thought, 'That's it.' It was my perfect outlet and I was determined to achieve this. I had been dancing from a young age and also at school but until now I hadn't seen it as a future career. But the difficulties caused by my dyslexia meant I very much wanted to prove myself.

When I was 13, I passed a three-day audition to get accepted into the Royal Ballet School but my skills were far behind the others. In my first year the older girls would look through a window laughing at me while I tried to copy the ballet steps of the others. I even burst into tears after my disastrous first-year exams. It did seem to take me longer to learn in those early days – but adversity does drive me forward. A year later I suddenly made an improvement in my dance. I had developed a real hunger to succeed and an obsession with being a ballerina. It was like the door to my future had opened.

I was still having problems with my GCSEs. I always thought the clever children at school weren't doing any work but of course they were. As soon as I realised this, it occurred to me that all I needed to do was put in extra hours. Then I could keep up. This gave me a new work ethic, which really helped.

One GCSE I desperately wanted to do was History of Ballet. I was told not to go in for it as I wouldn't pass but I thought, 'You can't say that.' Being as stubborn as I was, I took the exam and passed it anyway. Again I had shown myself I could achieve; things could happen for me.

I became more anxious about my dyslexia when I was 18 and out in the 'real world'. I felt as if I'd lost the protection of school and people would notice more. I hated the pressure of having to write a cheque in front of someone. I wondered how I could pretend I could do this and hide my problem with writing. I decided to memorise spellings I would have to use every day and used tricks to keep those spellings in my head.

I had once been told my ability to read would only reach that of a ten-year-old, but I was determined to achieve more. My mum had always said to me, 'You can always prove people wrong.' I had the frame of mind to do whatever I wanted to do. I would never give in. I was also clear that life isn't all about academic grades. I still had ways of doing well.

My own difficulties at school have left me acutely aware that today there is an unbearable pressure on children to achieve top grades. I hope that children also know that they all have different strengths – and maybe it can sometimes be harder for the kid who is good at everything to spot what their passion is.

There are so many different jobs out there and so many ways to achieve in life. With our children we must look at their strengths, not just their grades. We must encourage them to go with what they are passionate about instead of trying to expect them all to be the model pupil.

Looking back, it was my relationship with music, dance and movement that helped me gain the strength to get through the difficult times. It was a way of letting out emotions and expressing myself, which I may not have been able to do in words. It was an escape. I feel very fortunate to have found the profession that I was passionate about, and I recommend dance for children everywhere. After all, we know that if a child doesn't have exercise they don't learn as fast. We are meant to move.

Communicating in creative ways is becoming tougher and tougher for children because of the dominance of iPads and computer games. Dance helps us to express ourselves without inhibitions and understand space and physicality while building our confidence. I remember, at primary school, three or four girls in a corner planning a dance routine at playtime. They were always there working on their moves and I always thought how cool they were.

Dyslexia still affects me sometimes, but only sometimes. I have a phobia of academic learning, though I am currently trying to learn French. This is increasing my confidence, especially because ballet terms are always in French and so I know them already.

I do a lot of book signings and sometimes I freeze when someone gives me a name to write. Luckily people's names are spelled in so many different ways now so I can say, 'Do you spell Annabel this way or that way?' People do look at me strangely sometimes and then I might say, 'I'm so tired now I can't even spell my own name.'

I have to read through scripts for TV presenting, especially if I am pre-recording. I try to stick to talking about dance, which is what I know and what's been bred into me so I feel very at home doing this.

If I'm reading scripts in front of people I don't know, I explain to them, 'This is not my forte.' When you're young saying that kind of thing matters. We want to fit in and don't want people to notice we are different. But now I am older I have the confidence to say I don't understand something.

I would advise any child with dyslexia not to let the label make them think it will always be an issue. You can always surprise yourself and surprise others. It's not going to matter nearly so much after school. You have to go through the grind and if anything it will make you a stronger person than the person who has all the reading skills. One of my philosophies of life is always to work difficulties into my favour and find a way round them.

For me, in my life, dyslexia has been a little bit of a blessing. It helped me find my strength and directed me towards what I really wanted to do. Work hard, be focused, appreciate your strengths and you can always, always prove people wrong.

When a director is talking about a script I can visualise it all. I'm able to say, 'We need to add something here, something to keep things moving.' I put that down to being dyslexic.

Brian Conley

Entertainer, actor and singer. Struggled so much at school he thought he would end up a tramp. Learning his lines is never easy, but he is a huge success on TV and in musical theatre.

When my father died about ten years ago I was filled with grief. I went to see a counsellor and one thing he did was to help take me back in time to my school days. I remembered being in class and we were all getting up to read, everyone taking it in turns. The teacher was getting angry – we must have been misbehaving – and I knew it was getting to my turn and I knew I wouldn't be able to do it.

The counsellor told me to stand behind this young boy, which was me as a child. He said, 'Put your hands on the little lad's shoulders and tell him how you feel.'

I did this and I couldn't speak. I stood there and bawled my eyes out. I was in my early forties then and the pain from all those years ago was still there. I could vividly see what the teacher looked like, what the room felt like. The counsellor said,

'Why don't you have a word with the teacher?' I took the teacher 'outside' the classroom and told her how much she'd upset me and how it had affected me all my life and that she shouldn't have been so hard on that small child.

When the counsellor asked me why I'd taken the teacher outside the room, I told him, 'I didn't want to upset the other kids.' That's how real it was. I completely and utterly believed I was there, in my childhood, with all those emotions I had bottled up for all those years.

School days were hell for me. I can remember being in a writing lesson when I was five or six and having to write the 'a' and the 'b' between two lines on a page. I felt so confused. I didn't know how everyone else was able to do it and what was wrong with me. I desperately tried to keep up.

I was put into the remedial class. We would be trooped out of lessons and that was tough because we'd get picked on by the other kids. I would try to laugh it off but it really affected me. I couldn't get to grips with the maths, reading or writing. I assumed I would end up being a tramp because I was thick. Everyone else was getting on with it. What other answer could there be?

My parents knew something was up. They were worried, really worried, that I would sink. They also did wonder if I wasn't putting in the effort. But if I was in any exam, and I didn't have many, I just used to see them all sitting there writing and I felt as if I'd been beamed down from another planet. I sat there thinking, 'What on earth is this gobbledegook I'm looking at?'

The teachers didn't understand. They thought I was thick or stupid or not trying hard enough. In the end I gave up. I did go to school but I would be trimming the trees, looking after the smaller kids, sorting out the school milk – anything to stop me going to class.

Instead of working on schoolwork, I decided to work on making people laugh. This was my way of defusing the situation and hiding my lack of self-confidence and it became the thing I was good at. It also helped me develop this bravado which masked the fact that I knew in my heart there was something wrong with me. I had a strong singing voice and that, along with the jokes, meant that even at this early age I was disguising my weaknesses and forging my career path.

My mum and dad said to my music teacher Mrs Griffith, 'We don't know what to do with him,' and she replied, 'I want tickets to his first television show. He's got something. Nurture it. Send him to stage school,' which they did.

When I finished school at 16, I lied about my age and got my first real job as a Bluecoat at Pontin's Holiday Camp. Then I fronted a comedy show band and played in pubs and clubs. I was spotted and became a warm-up act for TV shows and then progressed to being on the shows myself. I went on to have my own comedy sketch shows and variety shows on ITV and started playing the lead in West End musicals from **Me and My Girl** to **Jolson, Hairspray, Chitty Chitty Bang Bang** and **Barnum**. I was also in the TV show **The Grimleys**, which was very popular.

I wasn't diagnosed with dyslexia until I was 27. This was a revelation. I remember dreading the tests. I thought I would be sat in a room and forced to read and write but it was much more scientific than that. When they told me I was dyslexic I realised that this was the answer. It was what I had been struggling with all my life. I was blown away.

Of course this didn't mean I stopped struggling. I hadn't realised when I started out on a showbiz career just how much you have to read and how many lines you've got to learn. Some of my worst times are the read-throughs actors have to do when we first start a production. You all sit down round a table and it's the first time you've met everyone and I struggle to read what's in front of me. Words pop into my head and I get anxious and it can get worse and I go into a downward spiral of panic.

I always work hard to try to understand the script before I meet the others. I remember, many years ago, auditioning for a part in a panto. I had been told I was going to play Blackbeard's partner, Scarface, so I'd learned all the words and went to the read-through. When I got there they said, 'No we've changed things. You're now playing the bosun.' I was sitting next to these wonderful comedy actors I really admired – Bernard Bresslaw, Anita Harris – and I turned the page and the first big monologue was the bosun's and I absolutely died. I struggled through the passage, hating every moment.

I always pride myself on working very hard and getting to know every word of a script. By the second day I know it. I have had to learn incredible amounts of dialogue. I've just done **Barnum** with lots of tongue-twister songs. When I have enough time I can do it. I have had to turn down **EastEnders** because of dyslexia, though. The quick turnaround and the scenes that have to be done that day would be too much for me to learn quickly. If I was there I would live in horror at what I would have to do. I need much more time to learn all my lines and go through them painstakingly. I recently hosted a TV series on Sky called **Timeline** and I had to be very upfront, saying, 'I'm dyslexic. I have to have time.'

I think being dyslexic and the fear of becoming a tramp is what drove me. My success is my way of telling the world I'm not thick.

I look on dyslexia now as a total gift. When I was growing up we lived in a council flat in Kilburn, north London, so I didn't come from a background with a lot of money. Without dyslexia I would probably have been a very good lorry driver, and there's nothing wrong with that, but thanks to dyslexia I have been able to pursue my dream. I have a real gratefulness deep in my core.

Dyslexia has given me the strength to take the knocks along the way, to face tough crowds in the working men's clubs. It helps me think outside the box and see the bigger picture. When a director is talking about a script I can visualise it all. I'm able to say, 'We need to add something here, something to keep things moving.' I put that down to being dyslexic and being a visual person and to knowing intuitively what the audience wants. Comedy may not win Oscars but to make it look easy is a real art.

When I had the help from the counsellor after my dad died and I addressed that particular moment at school, I think I let go of some of my anxiety about reading. I seem to have become much better at it as I have got older. I do read quite a lot now – I just have to put more time in.

One of my daughters was diagnosed with dyslexia when she was very young. We were 'on it' straight away. She had been at a private school with straw boaters, all very Victorian, and when she got to six or seven we realised it was all too academic for her. So we've moved her and she has shone. Everyone has a gift, I really believe that, and hers is organising. She can sort things out so easily. I can imagine she will shine in a job that involves those skills.

Unlike me, she gets more time in exams. School work can still be tough for her but she works so hard. It's difficult because she sees that her younger sister breezes through. We don't mind so long as we know she's worked hard. She's great socially and we are always happy to help her along.

I would advise her and all other children with dyslexia to appreciate and enjoy the fact that you're different. Embrace the fact that your mind works differently. You are looking at life from another angle. You're not part of the norm and that can be a real bonus in this world. Einstein – the world's greatest thinker – was dyslexic. I read that he didn't speak until he was eight and failed his university entrance exam. How amazing is that?

Schools can sometimes just bash out robots. I know it can be lonely being different and you may not always fit into the system but you will find something – maybe not straight away, but follow your heart. We are living in a visual world. If there is a block where it comes to writing then focus on what you're good at and find the help that's out there now to see you through. Try out the different fonts and the plastic overlays and the spellchecks. You've coped up to this point. You'll cope in the future. I was lucky that I found there was something I was good at and you will find that too.

There are many positive things about dyslexia. It certainly makes you more resourceful and it makes you think in different ways. I come across a problem and I circumnavigate it and take a different route.

Sophie Conran

Runs the highly successful, award-winning Sophie Conran homeware brand, sold across the world. Felt she was failing at school but at home she learnt about life's vast possibilities, which gave her the confidence and drive to succeed.

My parents are hardworking, entrepreneurial and always open to new ideas. My mum, Caroline Conran, is a cookery writer and my dad, Sir Terence Conran, is a designer and businessman. To me, as a child, they were inspirational. They still are.

There was always a lot going on at home. We had interesting people coming in and out of our house and there was lots of cooking with fresh ingredients from our big vegetable garden. At one stage we moved from London into this big, old, falling-down house which they put back together again over many years. We were living on a building site and it was both fascinating and wonderful to see something so decrepit brought back to life. It was a clear signal to me about the possibilities life has to offer.

I was especially lucky to grow up in a household that was visual. There was often talk about design. We looked at different products and appreciated their colour, form and function. I learned what makes a great atmosphere. I also learned about inventiveness from my mum. The way she cooked with food was, in a way, like writing music: she would take different elements and put them together in an instinctual way to create something new.

I felt at the heart of everything that was going on at home and of everything that the family was doing. I see this as my education and I was very fortunate to have it.

My education at school was another story – a story without correct spelling or punctuation. I still can't do either. I do a lot of writing and, thankfully, I have someone who works with me who can make corrections and check everything makes sense from a grammatical point of view. At school getting these things right was one of the criteria of success. In fact it was such a focus at my school that I felt I was failing in nearly everything.

I remember one teacher making us read out loud. She would point to us and get us to stand up and read a passage from a book. When it was my turn, all the blood would drain out of me. The words would look like they were dripping down the pages like wet paint. The letters would move around; they never stayed still.

When I think back to those times reading out loud I can see the classroom, I can see the desk, I can feel the uniform…this was my worst nightmare as a child. There wasn't anyone I could go to at school who could take up my cause. There wasn't any structured support for people struggling. They saw that I wasn't stupid but I was failing.

My favourite subjects were biology and history and I had fantastic teachers for these who brought what they were teaching alive. With the rest, the teachers would write on the board and get us to copy it down and nothing would stick in my head. I just thought I was thick. I was frustrated with myself because I couldn't understand what was going on. I think I lost respect for the school and its rules. My timekeeping became poor, I became a bit disruptive, I was off in the clouds, daydreaming and not engaged in what I was meant to be doing. I thought, 'I'm trying my best and I'm just being told off about it,' and I became rebellious.

The teachers were also very frustrated. Most of my reports said I wasn't trying hard enough. Then one of the teachers suggested I might be dyslexic and when I was 16 I was diagnosed. I think I was given an extra ten minutes at the end of exams, which was all there was on offer, but by then I'd had enough and wanted to be in the real world.

I don't think my parents had been overly bothered by my school record. I got ticked off a few times by them but not massively so. I think they could see there was more to me than what was happening at school; they just wanted me to be happy.

My dad hadn't been a high achiever at school – I think he is probably mildly dyslexic himself and I think my brother Jasper is too – but my mother is very academic and she had tried her best to help me. When I was younger I worked with her, filling endless little books with letters because my writing was terrible. She really tried but I would just end up in floods of tears.

I had always been very easily distracted. I remember watching the news on TV when I was young and not being able to follow the story because I was thinking about the person reading the news: what kind of day he had had, what he had been eating, why his skin was that colour; trying to work out who this person was, what his life was like, rather than listening to what he was saying.

I couldn't wait to leave school. I had a very strong group of friends and we had lots of adventures, which made it fun, but the whole point of school is to learn something and come out with lovely skill sets and I didn't.

I could read but I didn't ever pick up a book for enjoyment. It was always a slog. Eventually when I was an adult I found authors I was interested in: John Steinbeck was the first. Then I started reading more, but even now I still need peace and quiet and space and not to have a mind busy with other things.

We are all different and, for me, what's failing in the education system is that it wants everybody to be the same and until they recognise that people aren't all the same, a huge chunk of people are going to fail and leave school believing they are useless.

I still don't have confidence. I can still feel that failure. It's not awful; it's just part of who I am. Life's difficult for everyone so I don't think it's better or worse for anyone else.

When I left school I had quite a lot of different jobs. I was lucky because I went to work as a buyer for my dad and also with my brother Jasper's fashion team but most of all I was lucky that I had their entrepreneurial spirit in my blood!

Then I met my husband and became a mum and that changed things for me. It was the first thing I felt really good at. I took quite a lot of time out to be with the kids and be funny and creative with them.

I decided I wanted to have my own business and spend more time at home. I started a pie business; I wrote some books about pies; I worked with magazines. Some of the businesses worked well and some didn't but I'm a believer that if you're not making mistakes you're not learning anything. I don't feel any of the time was wasted because everything I had a go at has led to what I am doing now, which is a huge success.

I run my own homeware brand and my products can be bought in 55 countries. We make items especially for the home and kitchen – china, tableware, glass, crystal, cutlery, wallpaper, textiles and also gardening products. We've won a lot of awards and John Lewis is our biggest customer. We've especially had big success in America and Canada.

Detail is important in what we do. I take all aspects of a space or a product and then consider what it makes me feel and what I want it to make me feel. I design a lot of cups and this always begins with me asking myself, 'What do I want to feel when drinking a cup of tea?' It's a little moment for myself. It's a moment of peace, but then there are all the practical aspects of design that come on top of that. Everything is thought through. My goal is to make lovely things that bring a little bit of beauty and tranquillity and make people feel good.

In my work I put together lots of ideas and think about my emotional interaction with the product. I do this at home too. My kitchen's bright pink which sounds like it shouldn't work but it does. It is a family space, a happy space, a busy creative space and the colour enhances all of these aspects. When we come down in the morning and walk into the kitchen it's very difficult to be in bad mood.

My lack of confidence mainly shows itself when I am asked to do public speaking. People want me to do a talk or a cookery demo. I say to myself, 'You can do this,' but I can't. A strange thing happens when I'm stressed – I go deaf. My ears shut down. My doctor said this isn't possible but it does happen. I think it's because I'm not breathing properly.

Sometimes people still laugh at my spelling and think I could learn to do it if I just pulled myself together. They think it's ridiculous because spelling comes naturally to them and it's such a basic thing.

At school I was friends with the brightest girls who would help me and do my spelling tests for me. As a result of this I learned to surround myself with bright people in business. I don't cheat, as I did in some tests at school, but I do know how to use other people to help me find solutions to problems and this is invaluable.

There are many positive things about dyslexia. It certainly makes you more resourceful and it makes you think in different ways. I come across a problem and I circumnavigate it and take a different route.

I am pleased I am dyslexic. I'd like to be able to spell and be more numerate but I have people around me to help.

Some people think it's not useful to pigeon-hole people with terms like dyslexia but I don't agree. It's something that makes me different. Once you have a name for it you can answer questions about it, learn to work with it not against it, and move on.

…people with dyslexia…shun what they can't
do and they will fight and concentrate on
something else and prove the others wrong.

Kelly Hoppen MBE

Interior designer. Hated school, struggling with reading, spelling and maths, and left at 16 to start her own business. She had gained self-belief from her parents and uses her natural abilities to design homes, super-yachts, French châteaux, hotels and more.

According to my mother, I was always rearranging the furniture when I was young. My parents would go out, come back and I would have moved a wardrobe! If we stayed in a hotel I would shift everything around in the room. I always knew what 'worked'. It probably drove them mad!

I also loved show houses and flats and would get my mum to take me round to look at them at weekends. I loved the styles and the designs and seeing how furniture had been positioned and I learned from that. Then I'd go home and move things there.

This, to me, is a good example of how learning can happen wherever you are. It shows how important it is to follow your passion and your gut instinct for what you should do in your working life.

I don't remember my very early school days. I just know that I hated school. I didn't know I was dyslexic, I just thought I couldn't read properly, my spelling was atrocious and I was terrible at maths. I felt I was different from the others. I did excel at music, art and storytelling but kids can be very cruel when you have some kind of difference.

I think my mum was anxious for me and she would make me read out loud every night. She was amazing and she thought it would help but it was the worst thing she could have done because I felt 'put on the spot'. In those days no one knew to look for signs of dyslexia.

One thing my mum realised, through instinct, is that I would probably be able to memorise something if she drew it or if she linked it to a story of something that had happened to me. Without knowing I was dyslexic she did what a lot of teachers who work with dyslexic children do, which is to associate what I was learning with a picture or something else to help me remember.

My mum and dad didn't put pressure on me. They saw I loved designing and backed me. So I grew up with self-belief, and if you believe in yourself then others will too. I came from a mixture of a bohemian, artistic and traditional background. We had a wonderful life travelling and going to museums and galleries and doing all the things that fed me, including literature and theatre. I was very happy at home, I just hated school. I never talked about it to my parents until much later on in life, though I used to bunk off school because I didn't want to go and some of how I felt came out when I was caught.

I was terribly bullied and it made me feel very sad and alone but it was so long ago and I really couldn't care any more. It didn't affect my confidence because I left school at 16 and told them all to sod off and started my own business. That's partly what can happen to people with dyslexia. They shun what they can't do and they will fight and concentrate on something else and prove the others wrong. Actually I have probably achieved more than I would have had I not had dyslexia.

My father died tragically and suddenly when I was 16 and I inherited money. I used it to buy a flat which I did up and people saw it while they were visiting. From there my business developed through word of mouth, out of that passion I have always had for homes together with an interest in people. I have always loved textures, fabrics, smells and colours.

My first job was fitting a small kitchen for a friend of my stepfather's. Then racing driver Guy Edwards and other high profile friends who I knew through a friend asked me to design their homes. Other clients have included the Beckhams, Gwyneth Paltrow and Sir Anthony Hopkins. I've done interiors of super-yachts, hotels, restaurants, BA First Class Cabins and French châteaux. I've worked on houses all over the world and have written books that have been translated into many languages. My style is well-known: East meets West with clean lines and neutral tones. I can get inspiration when on holiday, from different cultures, when at an exhibition, with a friend, when I'm having some 'down-time' or just walking down the street.

I provide a personalised design service for all my clients. They fill out a huge questionnaire so I get to know the smallest elements of their lifestyle. This attention to detail is vital. I think getting to know the ins and outs of their lives is extremely important in order to create their family home. I want to get into their heads and learn what they want. The way the design looks evolves from there. I design a feeling and a look, and then focus on delivering on time and within budget to create the client's dream.

I also think creatively in other ways as I am an entrepreneur. One example is that during the recession I worked in countries where the economies were stronger.

I believe that if you are good at something, and I was good at design, you gain the confidence to overcome all the things that made you lack confidence. The things that you weren't good at become subsidiary because you start to make money at what you are good at. You end up forgetting about the rest of the challenges.

Dyslexia does still affect me. I am unable to add up in my head. I speed-read but that isn't a good thing as I end up skipping what's important. When I received my letter telling me I had been awarded an MBE, I remember reading it so quickly I missed out all the important details and had to go back and really concentrate.

If I really need to focus on something, I can't have any distractions, such as music. I just need to focus solely on that. If somebody's reading to me, I still have to do my best to concentrate otherwise my mind wanders and I am three steps ahead with a billion questions before they are halfway through as I have such a fast, creative brain.

In the past my staff would literally take months to work out my e-mails because my spelling and grammar were so confused! Sometimes my partner John will send me back a text I have sent him, saying he doesn't understand a word and when I read it back neither do I! All I can say about that is, 'Thank God for spellcheck.'

To this day I can't write down a business card on to my computer, however carefully I try to copy it. I was at a wedding sitting next to Charles Dance who is also dyslexic. I said, 'Let's exchange numbers.' He said, 'Give me the phone you'll get it wrong,' and I said, 'And **you** won't? We'll probably never speak to each other again,' but we did!

I've had no formal training for the work I do. My designs happen in my head as I am so visual. I also find I learn a great deal from speaking with others. My attitude is always that there is something to gain from a conversation. I talk to people, ask for help, get knocked down but then will get a yes. Working with others also makes me make different decisions about my own businesses and I learn even more.

Also I love sharing my knowledge. I have established the Kelly Hoppen Design School in London. I love seeing students' skills and confidence grow. I am an ambassador with the Government's UK Trade and Investment organisation. I have spoken a great deal to people who are trying to develop business and export. I always try to look at what it is that they are trying to sell to help them find the one hook which will grab attention. Sometimes people are looking at the bigger picture and how to make money but success can be more about your messaging as a business and how you get this across.

I remember one man who wanted to export British-made, horse-hair beds and I asked him what the story was behind them, what was the history, what was the fun bit about it all which was going to be the hook for someone to want to buy his product more than someone else's. That's what we worked on.

The Prince's Trust helps young entrepreneurs start up their own businesses and the way I work there is similar. Again, I ask people to look at the back story. I ask questions that are beneath the surface of the business plan. In fact I use this strategy in my day to day life. When I was on the BBC's Dragons' Den, I liked to know all about the person behind the product, I wanted to see their passion and then do my best to help them become successful and happy.

I use mind maps when mentoring others and in my own life. I start with a huge piece of paper and a single idea in the middle and branch from that. It is quite interesting to see how many ideas you can create that stem from one thing. Suddenly you find a little off shoot and it's a whole new idea and a whole new mind map is needed. It is a way to open the mind and be creative. I also find that I can surprise myself with the things I can think of when I'm just sitting relaxing.

There are ways to teach kids with dyslexia, and patience is key, but confidence in anything you do in life is always going to help you. Without it you can be pushed to one side. An important part of my life is to help others believe in themselves.

So when my daughter Natasha was diagnosed with dyslexia when she was four or five I was there 100 per cent supporting her. I went with her when she went to do her test and I was tested too which was the first time I was officially diagnosed. These days the teachers know what to look for and Natasha couldn't spell and was reading back to front. A wonderful teacher called Miss Petty helped my daughter and in the end she has excelled and is brilliant. She has set up her own business and is successful too.

I have achieved a huge amount in my life and I am very proud of it. Dyslexia isn't a disability, it's a challenge. You have to find your other strengths which the other children won't have because they're not dyslexic. Look on it as a challenge and you will overcome it.

I've turned dyslexia into a positive thing in the way
I work when I do stand-up. ...until very recently I
didn't write anything down. I would just improvise
my show over and over again and gradually craft it
into a shape. I call it 'verbal sculpting'. It means my
performing has this loose, conversational quality.

Eddie Izzard

EMMY award-winning comedian and actor; known for his distinctive stand-up routines, and acting roles including **The Riches, Ocean's Twelve, Ocean's Thirteen** and **Valkyrie.** Believes others with dyslexia at school suffered more than he did, while his determination pushed him forward.

For me, numbers were great, letters were crap.

I didn't know I was dyslexic at school. It was after a stand-up gig that a member of the audience came up to me and said, 'I think you're dyslexic.' Other people had also said to me that I had 'dyslexic traits'. They thought my mind worked in a dyslexic way.

I was interested and enquired about it. I have been tested twice and I have been assessed as 'severely atypically dyslexic' but in essence I think I am 'moderately dyslexic'. My spelling is all over the place, always was. That was the thing I knew was wrong. But I have always been very good with numbers. I knew my 12 times table when I was six.

I remember my mum helping me with early spelling tests when I was about four and them not working out at all. After my mum died, when I was six, I went to boarding schools. I sometimes had a difficult time at school and I wasn't top of the heap but I am kind of lucky because I am good at maths and I was in the 'A flight' – the top set.

My spelling was bad – cat written with a **k**, and ceiling written with an **s**. Why do we have a **c** and a **k** and an **s** when we only need a **k** and an **s**? I was intimidated by English literature and reading and I took an incredibly long time to read stuff as I sub-vocalise – I speak out the words to myself in my mind. Also, my writing was higgledy-piggledy. I remember trying to develop my signature, but all the letters were different sizes; it never looked elegant. My handwriting still annoys me.

So I always had lower marks in English and higher marks in science things. When the subject options came in when I was 16, I ducked out of all the subjects I couldn't do and I did A-level maths, physics and chemistry.

Dyslexia meant that one of the wheels on my wagon was down, but I have compensated for it. I have been given other attributes. I have a determination and a strong ambition to push myself.

I think there are a whole bunch of people who are creative and dyslexic, who suffered at school way more than me. When they leave school, they have to do something that is not to do with words. They form bands; they become designers, comedians, painters and actors.

I've turned dyslexia into a positive thing in the way I work when I do stand-up. When I write a show, until very recently I didn't write anything down. I would just improvise my show over and over again and gradually craft it into a shape. I call it 'verbal sculpting'. It means my performing has this loose, conversational quality.

I think regular people think vertically and dyslexic people think sideways. I have developed a way of thinking that goes forwards, but also I have a way of thinking around things. The connection between dyslexia and creativity makes me go off in strange directions and make sideways connections. I put things together that normally wouldn't be put together. So when a cat purrs I hear the noise and say it is drilling for oil. I call this 'imposing scenarios' – in other words imposing a different (and silly) scenario over a real one.

When I was tested, they said I had a slow processing speed and I think I do compared with other people. They showed me pictures and puzzles and they said I processed them slowly. There were certainly very bright kids at school and I didn't think like them. I was bright but not super-bright. I was street-smart, like a hustler.

Generally, if I do process something, I process it in a different way. So this means my conclusions are different from other people's. To me, learning French, German, Spanish,

Russian, Arabic is a positive thing to do for the world. It is good for humanity. If we learn languages it can help us work together more. If Europeans can learn to work together, other continents can see this and they can learn to work together as well.

The way I work is fairly logical, too, but not using straight up and down logic. It's a sideways logic, like doing gigs in French, which I think is a logical thing to do, but no one else is really doing it.

I was always intimidated by the written word and still find it very hard reading scripts. As an actor I put off reading scripts forever, which is stupid because how can I decide what I want to act in if I don't read the script? I have only recently started using scripts in my stand-up. It was a practical thing. In 2014, I did two months of shows in Germany, in Berlin. My brother, Mark Izzard, is my language teacher and we have the same sense of humour. I had an English show transcribed and my brother translated it into German and then together we tightened up the lines.

I have a certain weird confidence in speaking languages so I just smash in and often make mistakes. When you learn languages, I don't think you need to master the grammar until later. Communication is more important.

My theory about languages is that everyone is actually pretty good at speaking them, but the written part might obviously not be so easy. If you think about it: all French kids speak French, all Russian kids can speak Russian, all Mandarin Chinese kids can speak Mandarin Chinese. It's actually not that hard; it's just a case of endless repetition. If, in fact, you go and live in a particular country then you pick it up by trial and error. Deep immersion is the way to learn a language.

A lot of my personal confidence is the result of me coming out as a transvestite when I was 23. Attitudes in the entire world including Britain were so negative at that time (and had been for five thousand years): 'You're a freak…this is all wrong…don't tell anyone about it…just keep it to yourself…' When I stopped keeping it to myself and came out with the truth, overcoming that negativity led to the confidence I have.

This confidence has made me want to do things that are positive for me and, I hope, positive for other people as well. In 2020, I am hoping to go into politics. I feel humanity has to go forward in an inclusive direction or we won't make it. We have to get society working together and not pulling itself apart or we won't have a world.

Being dyslexic, my worry about politics is how much information I will have to read. I heard that JFK did a speed-reading course because there was so much stuff for him to read and I am worried about the exact amount I would have to get through. I tried to do a speed-reading course and then I couldn't get through it.

When some people read, they can read very fast but because I mentally speak out every single word to myself, this slows everything down. On the other hand, I've heard other people don't retain so much when they've read fast. When I read something, it does tend to stay in and I retain it well. I believe I can also see the logic (or lack of it) in arguments. I feel I can see how arguments flow in logical terms rather than trawling through printed words that will often seem to confuse the argument. I will have to throw myself into politics and see what I can actually do. It might well be tedious trawling through so much printed literature. In the first couple of years I will be curious to see what I will have to do to get on top of it.

At the moment, I read on my iPad by downloading a lot of books. The trouble is I read a certain amount and then, a few chapters into a book, I think, 'Oh, I might read that other book as well,' so finishing is difficult.

The only books I read as a child were the Narnia books. I did also read **The Hobbit** but only by listening to it being narrated. My brother and I recorded it from the radio and, if we missed a bit, my brother read that section out and we would tape it, so we'd still have a complete recording. So I had **The Hobbit** in my head and then I did go and actually read **Lord of the Rings**. I remember thinking it was a big chunky book before I started. It was intimidating going into it but then it became a page-turner and I had to find out what happened all the way through to the end.

I liked the end. The Orcs were taking over Hobbiton and then the Hobbits came back and kicked ass. They were no longer the kids from a village, no longer gardeners, but people on a heroic journey. Like the kids in the Narnia stories who became princes, another real heroes' journey.

I think in life we have to have a positive mission, because humans are good when we have a goal. We can all help the world to get to a better place because we can all do more than we think, even (or especially) if we are dyslexic.

As a writer, I often use the way my brain is
programmed to move a plot further forward,
or fix a section of script that niggles me.

Lynda La Plante CBE

BAFTA award-winning author, screenwriter and producer; creator of **Prime Suspect** and **Trial and Retribution**. Found learning to read and spell tough as a child. Believes that if you want to write a book, play or even a short story, start, keep going and have confidence in yourself.

At school I was described as a 'slow reader'. The reality was that I couldn't read at all. I recall being very confused about why I was unable to identify letters when they were chalked up on the blackboard. Up would go my hand and I would confidently say that the letter was an A and it wasn't.

However, if I was read to, I had an unbelievable memory and could appear to be reading fluently when I was actually either making it up parrot fashion or recalling the story.

I was fortunate to be a pupil at a very small school but, during my school days, dyslexia was never diagnosed. I had never heard of it and I doubt my teachers had. I was eventually caught out when I was found holding a book upside down!

My teacher, Miss Ash, spotted this and asked me to stay behind after class. At first she was very confused as to how I could remember whole pages of books. She then understood I had the ability to retain the written word but not to read or write it. She realised I was unable to differentiate between the letters of the alphabet and she produced a picture alphabet for me with the sounds of the letters – A with an Ape beside it, A with an Apple next to it. This meant I gradually learned how to read phonetically.

I was a great storyteller as I child. I used to spend morning milk breaks surrounded by a group of friends, telling them stories and always ending with 'to be continued'. I described a selection of strange creatures from fairy kingdoms who lived beneath rockeries and only came out at certain times of the day and night. I discovered that when one of the creatures had the name of a friend, they liked to hear more and more, especially if they were beautiful, magical, dangerous or exotic. My father used to keep a small folded-up piece of paper of one of my stories, not for the content but because he was astonished at the incorrect spelling and made-up words.

He found it very amusing, as it was as if I had created my own language. It certainly convinced him I would never pass my 11-plus.

I was always very happy at school and don't remember even the mention of the word 'bullying'. It wasn't an overly academic education, and the school felt it was more important to be able to fillet a fish and use the cutlery correctly. In the summer we would have classes sitting in the garden. I don't recall it ever being a very competitive environment. We had two elderly sisters who were joint headmistresses and they were very kindly and motherly.

I came from a very loving family and was cherished as a child. My parents encouraged me when I was growing up, although they were unaware of my theatrical hopes and later my wish for a writing career, so I am not really sure if they gave me any inner confidence.

Predominantly they simply wanted me to be happy. They were very proud, albeit often a little confused and would look at me with a quizzical expression that said, 'I don't know where you get it all from…'

I am an unusual combination because although I thought I was totally thick and stupid, and I learned very early on to hide this, I did also have this extraordinary and strange confidence.

My parents had never heard of the Royal Academy of Dramatic Art (RADA) but they allowed me to travel to London for an audition. I think my father, who was a salesman, thought RADA was a pub!

I was an actor for 20 years, appearing with all the top repertory companies and at the Royal Shakespeare Company, the National Theatre, on a lot of TV cop shows and as the ghost with hayfever who disappeared every time she sneezed on children's TV's **Rentaghost**. At drama school and when I was an actor I always got someone to read the script to me, which worked because of my extraordinary memory. Having someone read out the lines really helped me learn them.

I was reading fluently by then, but at times I could still misread scripts and I always found it difficult to replace a word I had mispronounced with the correct word. I once did a radio play and instead of reading out the word 'Hippolyta' I kept saying hippopotamus. Every time we got to that word in rehearsal I would find myself hesitating. It was almost as though I had frozen. After this I got someone to record my lines for me before I began to learn a script.

Another incident occurred when I was part of a chorus at the Old Time Music Hall. We had to sing, 'I know the Emperor of Japan, I've met the King of Spain I do declare.' The star of the show would then stride onto the stage, dressed in a top hat and tails, twirling her walking stick and continue the song in solo, 'In fact I know every public house, from Marble Arch to Leicester Square.' Because we had always rehearsed the whole song, including her solo, it was lodged in my brain and I found it impossible not to join in and the star was infuriated and demanded to know who it was in the chorus who kept joining in on her big entrance. It was excruciating because everyone knew it was me. I think being unable to stop singing was partly nerves but I also put it down to my dyslexia. Eventually the chorus boy singing next to me had to pinch me to keep quiet.

As a writer, I often use the way my brain is programmed to move a plot further forward, or fix a section of script that niggles me. This almost always happens just before I go to sleep. I start going over and over the storylines and if they don't appear to be logical – I like logicality – I iron out the problems and they are usually fixed by the morning.

When I began writing my spelling was atrocious. I see dyslexia as involving a fast eye movement so when writing I would put words in back to front, or completely miss sections out. Using a typewriter was when it all began to change for me. This was the biggest step forward. I never trained as a typist so I am self-taught but by slowly learning each key's position I discovered that I was beginning to be able to spell and punctuate correctly, and this was a major learning curve. I still occasionally made mistakes though. A producer laughed at a section of my TV robbery series **Widows** where I had repeatedly written 'porn broker' instead of 'pawn broker'. I hated the embarrassment and I also hated the fact that my misspellings were receiving the attention rather than the script. From then on I employed someone to proofread my scripts, or would ask a friend to check it over for me.

Another important development for me was my first computer, though I find all the automatic spellchecks and grammatical checks infuriating at times. I loathe the little wiggly green lines that appear in sentences to highlight grammatical errors. They drive me crazy and I become very impatient so I do ignore a lot of them.

I am now able to type at incredible speed as well as having support from the software. However, I still refuse ever to let any script, novel or document be sent without it being double-checked for mistakes, from **Prime Suspect**, to **Trial and Retribution**, to my latest novel, to a letter to Kingston Council about a parking ticket.

Accuracy to the smallest detail is vital for me. When I am doing research and interviewing people, from detectives to forensic scientists, I never use a note pad or tape recorder. I rely on my memory instead. I discovered that by making notes during a conversation it always unsettled the interviewee or stopped the flow and the same is also true of using a tape recorder. I think learning lines as an actor gave me a really strong ability to memorise entire interviews and even mentally edit them before I begin the writing process.

I still love writing. I usually start at around 9am after walking my dog in Richmond Park and write for as many hours as I can possibly do without being too tired to concentrate.

I would honestly say that for me the most vital contribution to achieving success with dyslexia was, as a young pupil, having a teacher who guided and helped me when I was struggling. I believe that these days schools are far too quick to label children with dyslexia and special needs. There's an eagerness to give children a label when they may simply just need a bit of encouragement and this can be very damaging to them in the long term.

It is imperative that anyone who is officially diagnosed with dyslexia does not take it as an affliction but as a positive step towards getting the help and support they need. It is one's own determination and focus that will eventually bring the realisation that dyslexia is not a life-threatening or humiliating condition. I have never come up against any 'brick walls' due to my now diagnosed dyslexia. I am hopeless with numbers, and even find it difficult to recall my own phone number, but it's not a major problem. I just keep phone numbers written in a book or on my mobile.

I do find that 'word blindness' is worse when using white writing paper and black or grey pencils, so I use coloured paper and pens. I also think it's interesting that a number of schools are diagnosing children with 'short term memory loss' as an indication of early signs of dyslexia. So here is a 'game' for young children to test for possible future problems: take a tray and place on it numerous small items such as a pencil sharpener, a wrapped sweet, a comb and a button. Allow the child to look over the tray for three minutes, then cover the tray. Wait two minutes before asking how many items they can remember. For the next round do exactly the same thing but ask for the items to be written down. The results are often surprising and heart-warming.

I think having dyslexia has never been foremost in my mind. I am a very visual person, keeping the faces of my characters in my head while I am writing. Perhaps having had the so-called 'problem' noticed early on in my school time, I simply overcame any issues it threw up.

It's important for everyone with dyslexia to learn they are not alone anymore. If you don't think about it, you worry less. You can certainly learn to cope a lot better. The key to overcoming dyslexia is not letting it dent your confidence. If you want to write, a book, a play, a short story – start, keep going and have confidence in yourself.

When you learn that it doesn't matter that you can't spell properly and you no longer feel humiliated about it – that's when you know you have come through.

Sometimes people hear [my business ideas] and think,
'Where did that come from?' … A lot of businesses are very
complicated – too complicated – and I try to simplify things.

Kenny Logan

Rugby player for Scotland and Wasps. Now co-owner of a sports marketing and events company. As a boy he cried with relief at the end of every school day. Learned to write as an adult, with the support of his wife Gabby and a special dyslexia programme.

Today I am not very good at reading and writing but, trust me, not being very good is an improvement. In the past I couldn't read or write at all. I would delete texts without being able to read them, just ignoring what was there. I would dread having an e-mail sent to me; I would always rather speak on the phone. I could never go to the doctor and fill in a form.

Recently I was talking to a big group of children in St Paul's Cathedral about dyslexia. They see a rugby player as being brave, but my message to them was that I hadn't been brave enough to tell anybody and I wish I had been. It's talking that got rid of my vulnerability, so don't be scared to tell people how you feel. I bottled it inside for years and years and years and that was what was so hard.

When you don't tell people that you can't read and write, they think you're stupid and a bit thick and they don't understand you. Now I tell people and they say they can't believe I've done so well.

I am proud of my rugby career and winning 70 caps for my country, but I think if I had been able to read and write I would have played better. I would have taken in information better and turned up to team talks and been able to process what was going on. I was never brave enough to go up to my coaches, Ian McGeechan or Jim Telfer, and say, 'Help me.' They would have understood.

I remember lots of team meetings for Scotland when instructions were handed out. My brain would overload with different messages. I would get confused and I couldn't concentrate. I would have been a better rugby player without all of this to deal with; without pretending I could remember what all the moves should be.

If there was ever a team meeting involving reading, I would turn up 15 minutes late and hide in the toilets. I remember Jim, one of the best coaches in the world, noticing my lateness and saying, 'He may be playing well, but he doesn't care.' I knew I cared more than anybody, but I wasn't brave enough to tell anyone my secret. I would pretend to read books during down-time when we were away on a tour, but in reality I was just staring at the pages. I struggled to fill in forms at immigration. I was given schedules but I couldn't read them so I had to keep asking questions. I lacked concentration on the rugby field and messed up simple moves while somehow coping with complicated ones.

I was a child of older parents; my mum was 40 and my dad 55. My dad was a farmer and his job was to work the soil, my mum's to bring the kids up. No disrespect to my mum, who was and always has been incredibly supportive, but I don't think people took as much notice of kids' learning issues in those days as we do now. I'm sure she would say the help wasn't available in those days either. I don't blame my mum because I didn't want to talk about my problems. No one did – not me, my teachers, parents or friends. I think everyone just thought I wasn't very bright, though I picked things up quickly on my dad's farm and I loved being on the sports field. They probably all thought I would be OK.

School was awful. For years I would have this horrible stomach ache, a dull pain inside me. Imagine a 16-year-old kid walking round with a six-year-old boy's anxieties in his stomach. I looked confident on the outside and was terrified on the inside. Words and letters confused me from the very beginning of primary school to the end of high school. I saw the other children progress while I was left drowning. I'd hear all these words and not be able to make sense of them or process them as they tumbled through my brain.

I struggled to copy from the blackboard, writing painfully slowly, repeating letters by accident. Everything distracted me. When I walked out after sitting my last exam I felt liberated from years of being in shock whenever I walked through the school gates. I felt free from the fear of saying and doing the wrong thing and showing everyone that I was different. Other kids knew I couldn't read and called me stupid, but I hadn't tried to get help. I had been waiting for the day it would all be over.

At the end of every school day, I would cry with relief as soon as I was out of sight of the others. Once, in frustration, I stood in front of the mirror in the bathroom at home and punched myself over and over in the head. I was frustrated and angry. I gave myself a black eye and told my mother it was from playing rugby.

The worst thing that happened at school was when I was 13. We had some questions written down and I said to the teacher, 'If you read these out to me, I can give you the answers.' She hauled me in front of the class and said, 'He thinks he can give answers to ten questions.' She read them out and I got nine out of ten right and I was so over the moon I went, 'Yes, yes,' punching the air. She said, 'Get out of this classroom. How dare you do that to me.' She'd thought I'd humiliated her but I thought I'd just proved I wasn't thick. I was filled with sadness and just thought, 'I can't wait to get out of here.'

I had a teacher called Deirdre Wilson who realised I was dyslexic who came to my house after school to help me. She told me what dyslexia was and she told me about bright people who are dyslexic. That helped me begin to believe I wasn't stupid.

One thing being dyslexic did for me was to give me the focus to concentrate on something I was good at, which was sport. If I hadn't been good at rugby, I would have been a farmer and would still be struggling. Because of rugby, I moved to London to play for Wasps. I married Gabby and met people who could help me.

Three weeks after I'd met Gabby she asked me to read an interview she'd done in a newspaper. I was completely stuck. I pretended to read it, but she was on to me. She quickly guessed I couldn't read and in tears I told her I was dyslexic. My fear was that she would break up with me, but of course she stuck by me and, when I was ready, she encouraged me to get help.

Gabby's my best mate and you listen to your best mate. I have the ultimate respect for her. She and my kids are everything to me. She made me realise there are lots of things out there to help. I didn't want to go back to any sort of classroom and 'try harder', but one day we watched a TV programme about a new technique for working with dyslexia, which involved physical exercises. I did feel more comfortable with that physical approach. The course has changed my life.

The course is now known as Step 2 Progress. It showed me that, if I tried to read, my eyes didn't follow a line smoothly but jumped about all over the place at different speeds. I was given balance and co-ordination exercises designed to strengthen a particular part of the brain and improve my balance. After a few weeks of these exercises I became disorientated on the rugby pitch and messed up my game, but I was told to keep going and then things got much better. My concentration improved and my eye tracking improved. Words had stopped leaping about and I could process them, and when I was 30 I learned my vowels – one of greatest achievements of my life. I know this treatment might not work for everyone but it worked for me and my self-esteem was stronger than it's ever been.

After I'd done the programme, I was the first to get to every team meeting. I was so confident. My whole image changed as a rugby player. Ian McGeechan said to me, 'You can tell me anything. How have you changed so much? Have you been taking drugs? Your attitude and the way you are playing are so different.' He couldn't believe how different I was. I told him about the programme and he arranged for other players to go through it to help their sport, which was brilliant.

I believe that being dyslexic has made my brain think differently. Because I can't do simple things I have to think of ways round them, and that is a strength.

I now run Logan Sports Marketing, a sports marketing and events company, with my business partner Paul Sefton. My job in our partnership is to bring business in and come up with new strategies and ideas. Sometimes people hear these and think, 'Where did that come from?' I think my brain works in a slightly different way compared with people who might have had more formal training or education. A lot of businesses are very complicated – too complicated – and I try to simplify things. When you do that, people who are very bright 'get' what you are saying and eventually others do too. If you look at the way the All Blacks play rugby, they play simply and well. They don't make many mistakes. If you complicate things it takes you away from the real focus.

Playing rugby, I didn't need to read and write too much. It wasn't required for my job. Now that I am in business, I have to read documents and write things down. I could never have done these things in the past. Having learned to read at the age of 30, I can now understand texts and respond to e-mails. I can see words and understand them, though Dictaphones and predictive text are very useful aids for me. Also, I am lucky to have a PA who understands my notes.

I wouldn't say dyslexia holds me back massively now. Sometimes I'm lazy and Gabby will say, 'You didn't read that properly' and I'll read it again. Because I'm not used to reading, I don't put the effort in sometimes, but I've just read Alex

Ferguson's autobiography and I enjoyed the read. I understood what he's trying to communicate.

When I was growing up, people believed that if you couldn't read or write you were stupid. Today people think differently about dyslexia, ADHD and dyspraxia. Now they want to help and they can catch it at six or seven years old or even younger. But even though there's more opportunity to get help, the threat to self-confidence and self-esteem still exists.

Catching dyslexia early is important because the more time you put into children when they're younger, the less concerned you need to be when they are older. If you can't read or write when you are 13 it's really hard for the future. You have missed out on a lot of your education. If it's noticed at age five, six or seven you can start putting the work in. This is the age when children want to learn. When they are older, if they are turned off, it's hard to get them back.

My little girl is reading like a 12-year-old at nine. My boy who is also nine doesn't enjoy it as much as my daughter, but he has a reading age of nine or ten. When he picked up a book for the first time and he was reading to me and I could see he wasn't dyslexic, that he wasn't going to hate school like I did, I felt amazing. But if he had been dyslexic I think I was in a better position to help him than maybe my parents were.

My message to children with learning difficulties would be to work as hard as you can and your mums and dads will respect you for it. A lot of parents don't understand what it's like to be dyslexic, especially when they're not. They wonder why their kids can't read when it comes naturally to them. They need to research what their child's going through so they can understand their children. That's what I asked Gabby to do when she knew I was dyslexic.

So go out there, get on the web and have a look at all the different dyslexia programmes. Schools need to help, but you can too. Try to stay calm, understand your child and don't be on their back all the time. And, don't forget, the more you can all talk about it, the better.

Dyslexia has made my people skills bigger and my personality bigger, of that I am sure. People say to me, 'You do the talking instead of the writing.' It's brought me the work of my dreams…

Meg Mathews

One time Britpop queen, now animal rights champion and vegan designer. Rebelled at school but loves the education she gains every day as she carries out her work.

I have been an interior designer, a party planner and a product designer, though in many ways I am best known for my social life as I was married to Noel Gallagher during the heyday of Oasis and Britpop.

I know I have been lucky because I've had so many great jobs but I am so pleased that, despite my dyslexia, I can use my experiences in life to help a cause I am passionate about and believe in to my very core.

I have spent some time recently advising the animal rights charity People for the Ethical Treatment of Animals (PETA) about celebrity liaison. This work was a perfect fit for me and added to my knowledge and passion for animal rights. When I knew I wanted to work with PETA I thought I would have to go to university to get qualifications as I have almost none. Luckily, when I went to see them, the people there said to me, 'Your little black book is your diploma and how well you get on with people is all the credentials you need.' I do find that people are more likely to take calls from me because they know who I am and that I know what life is like in the public eye.

My work included writing letters to people asking them to support PETA and they asked if I wanted to do one right away. I immediately saw they were using PCs and, like many people with dyslexia, I struggle with everything that isn't a Mac so I asked not to do it immediately.

Writing the letters was a big concern for me. Luckily PETA also wanted to make sure that the punctuation, vocabulary and what was being communicated in the letters was clear and accurate and the charity's messages were being put over clearly. So whatever I wrote was double-checked. This put my mind at rest.

I really don't like writing in front of other people so my way of dealing with it was to tell everyone in the office that I am dyslexic. I was always shouting out to people, 'How do you spell this?' I think they became used to me.

Spellcheck doesn't work for me. The other day I was trying to write 'accessorise'. Spellcheck gave up on me so I put it into Google and after 20 times of getting, 'Not found,' 'Not found,' 'Not found,' I had to ask someone else. Sometimes, if there's no one to help, I have to abandon a great word I've thought of and use something else instead, which is disappointing because I love words.

When I'm on the phone to someone and I'm writing things down, I find it very difficult when people tell me their e-mail address very quickly. I always say, 'Please could you either text it to me, e-mail me or spell it out slowly because I'm dyslexic.' It's very frustrating when it's incorrect.

When I tweet I do sometimes make spelling mistakes and I cringe for ten minutes but then forget about them. I also struggle with getting my 'b's' and 'd's' the right way round. I was taught to think of a bed and the b is at the end with the headboard and the d is at the other end and that works well and helps me get them right. Left and right I don't have a clue about so every time I need to know which is which I make an L with my left hand.

My background is in design and, before I worked with PETA, I was designing and producing bespoke wallpaper and scarves. Then I realised I couldn't work with scarves because they are silk and I found out the treatment of silkworms is appalling. I had been living with this image of people taking the little cocoons out gently but in fact they are thrown in a vat of boiling water. They are in agony. All animals feel and I believe that someone has to be a voice for them. Animals are not here for us. I have designed and launched a vegan handbag collection for Wilby, and I'm delighted about that.

One wonderful thing about working with PETA was that I learnt so much, which I never did at school. I learnt about factory farming, bullfighting and duck down in duvets. They are all incredibly cruel. The way the down is collected for a duvet or puffer jacket is horrendous, being plucked out of live geese and ducks. While at PETA, I helped them to try to get a zoo in Java closed down. It's thought that the staff there were stealing the meat in order to sell it, which was starving the animals. Since working there and learning so much more I've got rid of everything in my wardrobe made from sheepskin and goatskin. I would much rather not have it.

My interest in animals came from my mum. When I was growing up I always remember her being against veal and foie gras and in favour of animal rights. She never wore fur. She made sure I knew the names of every bird by going through bird books with me. I came from an ordinary background – my dad was a Scouser who was a chippy in the building industry and my mum was a secretary from the Isle of Sheppey – but my parents wanted an interesting life and moved over to South Africa for a year where we lived in a Land Rover. This means I can name every buck in the bush from a wildebeest to a gazelle to a springbok.

Even now I can't walk past a worm on a pavement without putting it on the grass. My daughter Anaïs says I'll never get my hair wet in a swimming pool unless I see a wasp struggling on the water in which case I'll dive in and save it.

I've passed on this passion. When Anaïs was younger someone from her school phoned me and said, 'You have to come here, Anaïs is hysterical.' I raced up there not knowing what was wrong and she said to me, 'The teacher just flushed a spider down the sink.' The teacher apologised and explained that the other children were screaming, but Anaïs was saying she would have saved it.

I didn't do well at school, though I did learn to read quite quickly. I thought, 'I'm not going to win academically, I will become a punk rocker, dye my hair and become a rebel.' I left with almost no qualifications but I do have people skills and I meet many people with none. They might have a master's degree but they can't hold a conversation. I find manners will get you very far.

Interestingly I was talking to an intern at PETA recently who told me he was dyslexic and had just graduated from university. He said he had received incredible support including a laptop, special help from a tutor and three weeks' extra time for his dissertation. He believed dyslexia is no longer a hindrance if you want to get an education and a degree, which is brilliant to hear.

After I left school I kept away from anything to do with writing. I was never a secretary or a PA. I did a Foundation Course in Graphic Communications and got into designing and printing. After my marriage broke down I started designing my own wallpaper and everything fell into place. Victoria Beckham saw a photo of my home in **Hello!** magazine with my wallpaper on the walls and rang me and asked where I'd bought it. I said I'd designed it and she asked me to design some for her. Life does seem to happen organically for me. When I was nine or ten, my mum said to me, 'What are you going to be?' and I said, 'I'm going to sing and dance my way through life.' There have been ups and downs but I do feel really blessed. I have my health, a beautiful daughter, a lovely house, work that I love and gratitude.

A lot of that gratitude goes to my parents who taught me to live my life to the full. It isn't everyone from my background who finds themselves sleeping under a Land Rover in Botswana at the age of 11. By nine I was eating avocados, passion fruit and guava, well before they were known in the UK. I remember visiting the Loire Valley and going from château to château when I was very young and also what it was like living on a wine farm in South Africa. I had so many adventures and different experiences throughout my childhood – my mum and dad really taught me that life was for the taking.

Because I didn't get the qualifications at school I had to choose a different path. I do believe I've had a lot of luck on the way. I've been to 10 Downing Street and I've met Bill Clinton, who is a vegan. The one person who left me tongue-tied was Dennis Hopper as I have found his films so powerful and meeting him left me lost for words.

Dyslexia has made my people skills bigger and my personality bigger, of that I am sure. People say to me, 'You do the talking instead of the writing.' It's brought me the work of my dreams – and it's been an incredible journey on the way.

I think it's because of dyslexia that I can see
something extra where most people will only
see one thing. Everything becomes a story.

Nigel McCrery

Author, screenwriter and creator of TV series including **Silent Witness** and **New Tricks**. He struggles to read even what he has written himself and says his first word processor was the building block for his future.

I am not well-read – I am well-listened.

I used to be a lorry driver and I bought tapes (that's what they were in those days) of hundreds of the classics: **Jane Eyre**, **Pride and Prejudice**, Dostoevsky, Agatha Christie. I would listen to them on my portable tape recorder when I was on a long trip. When I was a chauffeur and hanging around waiting to drive people home, I'd also tune in to the plays on Radio 4.

Even now, I struggle with reading and don't often try, still preferring talking books. I even find it hard to read what I've written myself. When I was a child my favourite books were written by Enid Blyton. I read all the **Famous Five**, **Secret Seven** and **Adventure** books. The prose is simple and the stories exciting. A godsend for people like me.

I see myself as educated by BBC Radio 4. My time at school, where I was meant to get my education, was grim. I was treated like a moron. The English teacher was a nightmare of a man. He used to come into our classroom, sit down and look at photographic magazines and teach us nothing.

I was in what was known as the second group and if we passed any exams it was a miracle. He resented teaching us and was in dispute with the headmaster and took it out on us. He was quick with the slipper and very quick with the cane. He would pick on anyone. He also took photos of the female pupils topless or semi-naked. I think when you're young a lot of things stay with you. The cane stops hurting after an hour, but the mental abuse sticks with you. I left school at 15, more than 45 years ago, and still resent the man, loathe him, even though he's been dead a good few years.

He is probably the nastiest character I have ever met – and I have been a policeman.

The school is now wonderful and caring and has special places for kids who need additional help. I oddly resent this, because I wish it had been like that when I was there when no one had heard of dyslexia. They invited me back and have named a specialist dyslexic centre after me, which is an absolute honour.

I wish my teachers had been better in helping me with basic English because my storytelling ability is very strong.

I needed help and was knocked back and I have never really recovered from that.

I had failed my 11-plus exam, which was why I went to that school. Family, for my mother, was one big long competition so this was the worst thing I could have done. My cousins had passed, were top of the class and went to university. My parents were of the era when, if your teachers thought you were dumb, they agreed with the teachers. I gave them no reason to think anything else. With dyslexia you begin to think everyone's better than you because they can write, they can read, they can spell. It gives you this inferiority complex, which is part of the condition, I think. I still feel I have that.

My parents despaired. I left school at 15 and my father got me a dead-end job at a Ministry of Defence establishment. I spent the first few years of my working life opening and closing large boxes in a freezing building. Then I got a stacker (forklift truck) licence before becoming a chauffeur and later an HGV 1 driver.

During that time I attended night school and picked up a few O-levels – English language, English literature, geography and history. Although my teachers were a different breed and very helpful, if they asked me to read out a passage in class, I'd say I'd forgotten my glasses so I didn't have to. Dyslexia teaches you how to cope with things and how to get round things.

Then I joined the police. I think they let me in because I was big and bulky and good for throwing people out of pubs. They were having real problems recruiting and I think they thought, 'Nigel won't be elevated above PC but he will have his place,' and that's what happened in many ways.

Dyslexia caused me problems as a policeman. During the first statement I ever took, I was falling apart. I was just so embarrassed about my spelling and punctuation. I could see the writing was littered with mistakes. From then on I 'accidentally on purpose' would forget to get witnesses to sign them. I would go home and completely rewrite them with a dictionary by my side. Then I would get my wife Gill (a very bright grammar school girl) to check them and correct any mistakes. I would then take them back into work the next day and revisit the witness saying, 'I'm ever so sorry – you forgot to sign this.' I would ask them to read it again, which was important, and then sign it. You can imagine if a defence solicitor had got hold of that! But it was quite innocent.

I began to realise I was dyslexic during the time I was in the police force, when I heard an interview on the radio with the actress Susan Hampshire (a long-time hero), who explained her symptoms. This made me careful with my children and I made sure they had extra help at school. One of my daughters is a very good writer and my other daughter has a very good degree. My son achieved ten GCSEs and two A-levels. However, he never liked school and is a diving instructor on a tropical island in Cambodia, so life can still be good.

If you exercise your right arm, it gets bigger. If you don't use your left arm, it withers. If you exercise the parts of your brain with imagination, it gets strong and that's what I think happened to me. When I listened to a play, I would think about the characters, imagining who they were. If it was **Pride and Prejudice**, I imagined what the ballroom was like, imagined what Mr Darcy and the other characters looked like. My imagination was working overtime. With tapes the imagination gets the same stimulus as if you were reading.

I retired from the police with an injury in 1987 and, at 35, was accepted at Trinity College, Cambridge, to read Modern History as a mature student. I think telling them dark stories of murder clinched it for me. For the first three months I didn't cope and came very close to leaving. However, the students and fellows were brilliant and pulled me through.

I also have to give a big thank-you to Sir Alan Sugar and his Amstrad 9512. It was, I think, the first dedicated word processor. I bought it from Dixons at the Broad Marsh shopping centre in Nottingham. I still remember that moment because it saved my life. It had a spellcheck and an unbelievably noisy daisy wheel printer. A year later I bought a sheet feeder which meant I didn't have to put the sheets in one at a time. It was wonderful, much better than a typewriter. If I didn't get a word right it put another one in for me. If it hadn't been for word processors I would never have been a writer. Now I have Word for Windows, punctuation checks, a thesaurus, English checks – and I'm surrounded by people who are cleverer than me to edit what I do. Heaven.

I was thinking of becoming a teacher but I didn't have GCSE maths, which you need. Cambridge had given me confidence so I wrote my first book, joined the BBC Graduate Entry Scheme and started work on some of their drama productions including **Our Friends in the North**. When they were looking for a new drama series, I came up with a series called **Back Up** followed by **Silent Witness** and they commissioned them.

I can write anything between 5000 and 10,000 words a day and I love it. I love the sense of putting it all down and never feel tired. I have written historical books: one was published recently on the Rugby Internationals killed in the First World War. I think it's because of dyslexia that I can see something extra where most people will only see one thing. Everything becomes a story. That muscle has been so developed. I see a story within a story. I was reading a book about the First World War that said, 'This is where the black pilot did such and such,' and I thought, 'What black pilot? There's a story there…'

As I said, I still find it hard to read even my own work. One year I agreed to appear at a literary festival. I later regretted it and got into a terrible state about it. Lenny Henry is a good friend and he phoned me up and said, 'For goodness sake, think about what you've done in your life.' It took a lot to calm me down but he did. Good guy. Even now if I go and they want me to read from one of my books, I say, 'I'm happy to come along and talk about the history of forensic science' (or whatever the book is about) 'but I'm not going to read passages from it because I'm dyslexic.'

I have a huge amount of anger within me. I am motivated by proving to people I can achieve a lot. It was a great driving force, especially until my parents died, and it still lingers within me. If you are angry and can channel it into something positive then revenge and anger can be useful.

Life for me is not about how many times you fall down, but how often you pick yourself back up. That's my attitude and it might be to do with dyslexia. You do get knocked back, for all sorts of reasons. Look at Frederick Forsyth and JK Rowling whose books were rejected many times when they started out and who became incredibly successful. In life you just have to keep getting up and if you do that, you will get there.

Dyslexia helps me in my football… My mind is always working ahead, thinking, 'If the ball goes there and there I will have a better chance if I move there.'

Steven Naismith

Premier League footballer, plays for Scotland and Everton. Though he resented it at the time, the extra help he received at school, together with support from his parents, helped him turn his education around.

One of my favourite things to do is to sit in a coffee shop and read a book. I have just finished training for the day and that's what I'm going to do this afternoon. When I was at school I couldn't think of anything worse than reading – it was daunting – so enjoying reading now is a great achievement for me.

At primary school I was always average or below average. I was really bad at reading and spelling. Every week on Fridays we had a spelling test and I was always one of the lowest scorers.

I remember at secondary school, when the teachers were reading a book in class, I would read the paragraph ahead in case they asked me to take over from them. If I had to read out loud I would stutter and stammer over difficult words and feel really embarrassed about it. One of the teachers noticed my difficulties and she suggested I get tested for dyslexia.

I never felt the brunt of bullying about finding schoolwork tough because I was good at football, which meant I was a 'cool' kid, but I can understand how it can be hard to handle. There was the odd time when I had to go out of class in English or when I got more time in an exam and I felt awkward when the others were asking me why.

When the school brought my difficulties to my parents' attention it made them much more aware that I needed to work harder to get through. They had got me an English tutor before we found out about the dyslexia to try to help me because I was falling behind. Extra English was not what I wanted to be doing with my time. Sometimes I saved my tutor's number on my mobile and told them she'd called to say she had cancelled when it wasn't true.

When we found out I was dyslexic they forced me to have extra help. I was very reluctant to be taken out of class but my mum and dad said I had to do it and it would benefit me. Now I am 100 per cent pleased. It meant I was more relaxed in my exams because I knew I had more time and I didn't need to rush. Dyslexia doesn't mean there's something wrong with you and you're not good enough, it just means your brain works in a different way and the diagnosis gave me an equal opportunity. Thanks to being diagnosed I went from being below average to above average.

I have worked very hard in my career and I think a lot of that comes from my school days and dealing with the challenges I faced there. I am not someone who ducks challenges, which showed in school and it shows in my football. As a young footballer I knew I had to work hard to maximise my game. I've had two bad knee injuries and, when you come back from them, your body takes time to adapt to get back to the performance level it was at before. I think I was able to focus so completely on my recovery both times because of the focus I learned at school.

One thing my job has helped me with is not caring what people think. I don't mean this in a bad way. If you're not playing well, it's not just the pundits who have a go at you but your own fans as well. Footballers have to have a thick skin and in life you need to learn to listen only to the people who matter to you personally. Because of this I'm not embarrassed about dyslexia and I'm happy to talk about it openly.

Dyslexia helps me in my football, I am sure of that. Some people say dyslexics can have better peripheral vision and think more creatively or 'outside the box'. People say I am good at timing – being in the right place at the right time –

and I don't think it's any coincidence that a lot of chances fall to me and I create a lot of chances.

If someone's watching me play and thinking, 'He's lucky to be in the right position on the pitch,' I would argue it is about more than luck. My mind is always working ahead, thinking, 'If the ball goes there and there I will have a better chance if I move there.' Thinking in this way is something I do naturally. In some situations off the pitch I consciously think ahead: is there any way to improve myself in what I'm doing – in reading, as an example. But with football it's all split-second timing and these decisions are made subconsciously.

It would be very interesting to survey everyone in British football to see how many are dyslexic. Footballers are all meant to be thick and not know much but I imagine a lot are dyslexic and it improves their performance, which is why they've achieved all they have. Dyslexia means you're not thinking in the way you're taught to think. It's just the way you are and it turns you into a different player.

A lot of people with dyslexia, including footballers, probably still slip through the net. One of the hardest things for a young person is to speak up and not be embarrassed. You don't say what you really believe because you're concerned about the reactions of others. As I've got older I've realised it makes me a better person if I am honest about these things. If kids are struggling they don't need to say so in front of a class, they could just talk to a teacher at the end of a lesson. Things could get easier for them and they can get the help they need which will give them opportunities in life.

My parents believed in me and encouraged me as a person. They strived to help me find ways to solve any problems in the right way, while making sure I kept my feet on the ground and didn't think I was better than I was, especially when I was doing well at football. I am a positive person and I look on the bright side. If there's a problem I think, 'Let's solve it and move on. Let's not mope about and feel sorry for ourselves.'

Dyslexia hasn't dented my confidence but I can see how it could have done when I was younger. I would work hard at school and not get any better. Being diagnosed has helped me maintain my confidence. If I had a bad day I would think, 'I'll make the next day better. I am going to be able to do this.' Thanks to my parents I never doubted my ability to succeed at something, whether it was an English essay or a modern studies exam or anything else.

From when I was 18 to about 20, I decided to focus on my reading. I was doing a lot of travelling with football and had many opportunities to read and knew I wanted to get better. I read any book I thought would interest me, mainly biographies, and would get through around three pages at a time. Later I did some work with Dyslexia Scotland and I've learned about different fonts and different coloured paper that help with reading. They've talked to me about different ways to improve my reading and make it easier.

I started enjoying reading more and I went from biographies to fiction. This is great because I can bring in my imagination. I read **The Girl with the Dragon Tattoo** and my imagination had made the book so good for me that I felt the film was disappointing and didn't do it justice.

Many boys are desperate to be footballers and don't care about their schoolwork. They need to look at the stats of the number of kids who make it through. When I was ten I trained with Rangers two nights a week and played for them at weekends. I left when I was 13 and I signed with them again when I was 20. Not one player was there who I had done the youth training with seven years earlier. They might be at other clubs but they are not where they thought they would be when they were ten. People think about the Premier League being the best in the world but, even there, footballers can make good money early on and then contracts dry up and they are back in the real world.

Schooling and education also forge you into the sort of person you are going to be. Respecting your teachers is part of treating people as you would like to be treated, including your parents who are the backbone to who you are when you become an adult.

If being a footballer doesn't work out there are so many jobs around the game, from sports science to dieticians. Football is a sport that has grown arms and legs and there are different and new careers which surround it and which require time at university, which is another reason to do as well as you can at school.

I'd like parents who have kids with dyslexia to know there is nothing to be scared about if you can get the right support for your child. Dyslexia can be positive. I have a young daughter and I know it is easy to worry about things but there is no reason to with dyslexia. With every year there is more awareness and more help out there. Your child is going to grow up to be creative and think differently. There will be situations when you're thinking of doing something one way and they'll say to you, 'Why not do it like this?' You'll see for yourself how amazing it is that they think in that way.

I think that kids with dyslexia look at the bigger picture more than the detail. I think this is why their imagination and vision is exceptional and it's something to be proud of.

Paul Nixon

One time wicket-keeper for the English national cricket team, and captain of Leicestershire Cricket Club, still working to promote the game. School was full of stomach-churning fear and distractions. Says special exercises for developing the brain helped him achieve as a professional sportsman.

My name is Paul Nixon and I am Hon Dr of Letters at De Montfort University. This honour was awarded to me for 'Outstanding Achievements in Cricket' but, that aside, I promise you no one would ever have seen it coming…

My school days were a challenge. I struggled with grammar and I remember missing school and faking illness to avoid spelling tests. I was phobic about them. The teacher would tell the whole class what we had all scored, which was real humiliation and I was kept after school for extra spelling lessons. I think the Cumbrian accent doesn't help the spelling. I get very confused with words that aren't spelled as they sound.

I also had this stomach-churning fear when I was asked to read anything out in class. I felt under massive pressure with my reading and my concentration levels were not good. I tried to read books but the information didn't stay in my brain. I would read one page, turn to the next page and then not remember what was on the page before. I just couldn't hold on to that information. In exams my mind would wander and I would go blank. It was as if I was in a trance.

Even the farming lessons were annoying because I didn't need to learn what was being taught – I was a farmer's son. I found that anything could distract me. I would look outside the window and watch the sheep, look at the birds flying past the window, hear someone knocking on the door or talking in class. All the distractions took up so much energy that there was no energy left for the lesson. Information from the teachers would rush through my head and out again. I had to do a lot of repetition to keep anything in there.

I think I was bordering on hyperactive, full of beans and energy. Luckily I got my self-esteem from sport: football, rugby, cricket, athletics and gymnastics. In my first year at secondary school I was playing fifth-year sport. I also missed lessons because I was doing basketball, cross-country or another activity. I always felt lucky that I was away a lot as it helped me brush away my lack of learning.

Apart from my school lessons, childhood was a fun time. I grew up in a small village in Cumbria and we would all wander down to the village school together. I didn't ever suffer from teasing or bullying because I was a big, strong lad, but if people had a chuckle at me in class then I would laugh at myself too.

I think my mum is a bit dyslexic so she wasn't a massive help with homework because she struggled as well. My dad was busy on the farm. My parents just thought I would be all right. The worst-case scenario was that I had a farm to go back to.

At 16 years old I played football for Carlisle United's second team but, in the end, cricket chose me. I had to work hard at rugby and football but I wasn't outstanding. With cricket I shone much more easily. When I played cricket for England Schools, I was one of only a few chosen to play a year early. Even with sport I had to be careful not to be distracted by a noise, a thought or someone moving.

There were 300 people living in my village. When I was 16, I left home and moved down to London, into a hostel in Hampstead with 700 others! I had been taken on as one of the ground staff at Lord's Cricket Ground to help me get a leg into the first class game. There were 15 or 20 of us doing duties around Lord's: cleaning windows in the Long Room, changing the numbers on the scoreboards as runs were scored and wickets fell, pulling on the covers and selling the scorecards to the fans.

I was quite overawed by it all. I had gone from being a big fish in a tiny world to a tadpole in the city. I remember having to buy new wicket-keeping gloves from a guy in Camberwell, south London, and not having a clue where I was going. I was always getting lost on the Tube.

Then I joined the Leicestershire team. Because there is only one wicket-keeper in a team, my only opportunity of being in the first team was when the keeper got injured. Looking back, I think even then I was a slow learner. The coach would tell me things that were going in one ear and out the other, such as which techniques to use with which bowlers when I was batting. I was full of energy and always asking questions but I was making the same mistakes over and over again. Then finally what the coaches were telling me would click and go into my working memory. Also, remembering where the other players were in the field was hard for me to remember and I had to keep checking that.

If I missed a catch or messed up in batting I would give myself really bad messages about my play, which would continue to distract me. My brain would be full of this clutter. Later in my career another cricketer, Jeremy Snape, taught me how to put positive thoughts before negative ones when at the crease and that did make things much better.

By 24 I had scored 1000 runs and was selected to join the England second team tour to India and Bangladesh. At the time they were looking for me to be the new wicket-keeper coming through for the England first team. Unfortunately I got injured and had to pull out and I thought that was it, I would never play for my country.

In fact it was not until I was 36 that I made my England debut – an age when most cricketers have retired. It was a great moment for me to achieve this and to prove something to all those who had doubted me. I am convinced that this finally happened because of a course I did with Wynford Dore who helps people deal with dyslexia through his Zing programme of exercises.

When I was tested by Wynford, he found out that my eyes were shuddering as they moved across the page. He said this meant that my working memory couldn't process what my eyes were seeing and what I was reading. I was given these co-ordination exercises and found that, after practising them, things could stay in my brain and my skills somehow became more instinctive and automatic.

I did six months of brain games and other exercises and noticed a real transformation. I had never read a book in my life before this but I bought a book about cycling and read it three times in just a few days.

If my wife Jen asked me to go to the shops for a loaf of bread I used to forget what I had gone out for and come back with all sorts of other things. She would say, 'Great – but where's the bread?' I was scatter-brained and would fail to post letters and pay bills. The exercises meant that life got easier. My thoughts slowed down and became clearer. I remembered more and more.

In my testimonial year I had a lot of functions to organise. The business side of things frustrated me and every e-mail took longer than it should. I still need spellcheck but everything has speeded up. After-dinner speaking had been very hard and I had been totally reliant on notes to keep me right. Now I can remember things so much better, I don't need many notes and I don't get nervous and wound up beforehand. I am in a calm place.

Looking back, dyslexia did have some advantages for me. My attention to detail was very good – being dyslexic you sometimes work so hard on your skills and in the gym that you lose count of what you have done and do more and more. Doing the extra reps and practice made it ingrained. I also had a way of looking at the big picture during a game and thinking about tactics in a different way.

I retired after 23 years playing professional cricket and the honour of being captain of Leicestershire and playing for my country. I now work for the Professional Cricket Association, looking after England's corporate clients, and I do media work and coaching. I am involved with the brain-training company ZingUp – the organisation that made a huge difference to me.

I am also setting up the Paul Nixon Cricket Foundation for 16–19-year-olds in Leicester, which will help them get through their BTECs in maths and English as well as their cricket. I come from a kind background and I know life is for giving.

I think that kids with dyslexia look at the bigger picture more than the detail. I think this is why their imagination and vision is exceptional and it's something to be proud of. I have always been involved with businesses and companies and I know that you do not always need great reading and writing skills to play a major role at work. With the right enthusiasm and focus you can do this with the skills you do have – but there is help out there for people with dyslexia too and that is a blessing.

...all my struggles had turned out to be an advantage. I found out after I left school that, whenever there were difficulties, I could deal with them. I had a mind that immediately knew how to look for solutions.

Theo Paphitis

The owner of stationery chain Ryman, homeware specialists Robert Dyas and lingerie retailer Boux Avenue, known to millions for his high-profile appearances on the BBC's long-running **Dragons' Den** series. After years in the bottom stream at school, a teacher suddenly saw his potential.

I started life in Cyprus and came to the UK aged six or seven. Then my only problem was not being able to communicate in English and needing to learn the language. Verbally, learning English was good. The problem came with reading and writing. My reading was incredibly slow and tortuous and my spelling was the spelling from hell.

It was very clear to me that I was struggling more than a lot of the others because I was always in the lower streams in school, with kids who didn't want to learn in life – which I did – or who had much less ability, so things didn't go well. In classroom debates and discussions I was up there and equal with the rest of them but, if anything had to be written down, it all went pear-shaped. I remember having a problem reading the questions and finding it hard to understand the meaning of a sequence of written words.

My secondary school was quite tough; it wasn't for the faint-hearted, especially in the lower streams where I didn't feel comfortable. 'Stupid' and 'dunce' were the common words I heard from the other children, which today would be called bullying. My main cohort of friends were in the higher streams, not in my class. The things that interested me were the things that interested them. But I was a determined individual so I tried incredibly hard. I developed this skill of finding ways of working round problems to get to understand what was being asked of me. I would have to spend a lot of time working at home. It would take someone else 15 minutes to do their homework and it would take me an hour and a half, but I would deliver it. I would plan; I would use crib sheets. What wouldn't I have done at that time for some electronic device like an iPad or computer to help me find out what I needed to know.

Fortunately for me, it was very much in my character to want to succeed. Because of that, I wasn't prepared to give up and I wasn't prepared to be 'stupid'.

Sadly, home life was complicated so there wasn't any direction or help there, but I did get a stroke of luck. After a couple of years in the senior school, one of my teachers was ill and the deputy head of year took the class. He was an old navy veteran, very strict and everyone was terrified of him. The class wasn't in his subject so his job was to keep us quiet for an hour and a half.

He sat there and talked to us about a variety of things. At one point he was talking about the Royal Navy and he asked if anyone knew how ships stopped. People put their hands up. Someone said, 'They put the brakes on.' Someone else said, 'They throw an anchor down.' I said, 'They reverse their engines.' He asked me why and I told him about the principle of momentum which I had basically worked out in my head. That simple conversation changed everything.

At the end of the class, the teacher asked me to go to his office. We had a long conversation and he called me in again. He had a chat with all my teachers and I was put up a set in maths immediately because I was already at the top of my maths class. I was good with numbers even then. He moved me up in English and I then got moved up in most of the subjects. In geography, the teacher was quite sympathetic. In fact I wished she was less attentive because it meant I stood out a little bit from the others, but I was happy to take the attention rather than failing. Not surprisingly I excelled in that subject and geography was the one exam I passed.

Most definitely the fact that the deputy head of year had believed in me gave me huge confidence. No one said, 'You're dyslexic,' as the term wasn't known then. What I knew then was that I wasn't stupid, I just couldn't cope. Suddenly someone else had seen it too.

I was encouraged to join the students' union and I became the school rep, which gave me a chance to show I had abilities outside the classroom. My union duties included thinking of ways to improve school life for the students. The school didn't have a tuck shop and I convinced the school they should get one. They gave me cash flow, a cupboard and a key to keep my stash and an area to sell it from. Incredibly, it worked like clockwork and I employed people to do some of the duties, which was a great way to stay warm in winter. It was harder to get helpers in the summer, though. The tuck shop was a big success. I thought of a lot of different ways of increasing the profits. I remember once weighing a box of crisps and telling the manufacturers there weren't enough in each pack and they sent me a free box!

I left school at 16 and got the only job I could get. I was a tea boy and filing clerk at a company in the City of London. It was a scheme paid for by the Government for people who hadn't worked before so it cost the business nothing. I felt miserable. It's not good to be a filing clerk when you're not good with letters. As an individual I was popular and I got on with everybody really well, but I did frustrate them with my lack of ability. It was clear that my career was not going to take off any time soon.

I decided I had to move on and I got a job in a shop selling watches in Bond Street. I was absolutely ecstatic and sold a Rolex on my first day! In this job there was lots of talking to people and dealing with numbers, and no writing. I wasn't struggling in that environment. I was doing a job that I was meant to be doing. All my competitive instincts showed themselves and I did very well there. I still buy my watches at that shop now.

In leaving school and going to work, I discovered the most wonderful thing. I found out that all the difficulties I had in school and all the things that happened to me there, plus all the things I had to do at school to get through the day, had taught me how to find solutions to problems. I could use this problem-solving skill to get ahead in business. When I went into the world of work it was quite a novelty for my employers to find someone of my young age who had developed that ability.

Others at school were taught and learned in a structured way. They understood what was being asked of them. For me, all my struggles had turned out to be an advantage. I found out after I left school that, whenever there were difficulties, I could deal with them. I had a mind that immediately knew how to look for solutions.

I had trained myself and I have found that, for other friends of mine who had suffered in similar ways at school, the vast majority have the same skill. It has become natural for them; an adaptation. Of course it's not true of everyone. Other people don't have the drive and ambition and take the view, 'I'm never going to be able to do this.' However, if you do have the drive, dyslexia becomes, later in life, a positive instead of a negative. Undoubtedly.

This is why I am attracted to companies that are doing badly and need turning round. When I see a problem, I can see a solution very clearly. I am happy to go and fix things.

Of course I do need a team around me, the people I call 'the professionals'. They have degrees from university in accounting and law and I employ lots of those. They are **ever** so clever.

Now, dyslexia is not a problem for me. In fact I have embraced it. My PA is sitting next to me right now and I ask her how to spell things. She's here to do that for me. And I can do things that other people find complicated in seconds.

When I was on the BBC's **Dragons' Den**, my dyslexia was an advantage. Someone was pitching a business idea and I was already four steps ahead of them while some of the other 'dragons' were lagging behind. I found I could see the sequence of what they were saying, dissect it and find the flaws in it a lot more quickly.

If you have confidence, I believe it is better to have dyslexia than another condition. When my eldest son was born we realised he had a similar problem. We had a diagnosis of dyslexia and this was a relief more than anything else. I knew I could get him help. I knew he could have a fulfilling life and I knew what he needed.

My message to anyone who's dyslexic and finding education a struggle is that it's just something you have got to accept within your make-up. The advantages of having dyslexia outweigh the disadvantages – not if you're in an academic setting and you may have to accept that this won't be your strong point. But that's no big shakes. I wouldn't worry about it. If you have parents who are hot-housing their kids then dyslexia does become a problem.

With my kids I presumed that, so long as they could read and write and were good people, then the rest of life would work well for them. Academia is not where it's all at. Once school days end, other doors open.

Once upon a time Mr and Mrs Smith, blue collar workers, struggled and saved to get their kids into a good school and into university to guarantee them a great job with a great salary and security. That brought social mobility. That's a lot of old rubbish now. A degree doesn't guarantee you a job now. Thousands leave university without jobs. There are apprenticeships out there that enable you to earn while you learn, rather than spending three years learning to think. Learn the skills on the job and gain an advantage, rather than getting a degree in thinking.

Of course academia is an advantage in sciences, medicine and specialist subjects, but I think in general subjects you are better off learning while you work. By the time the graduate leaves university after three years with no job, the others have moved up the pecking order.

The message from me is that with dyslexia there are more positives than negatives. Just don't put yourself in an environment where you will suffer from the negatives – put yourself in an environment that will help you benefit from the positives.

At school and in life you want to win everything all the time and sometimes you can't. Having dyslexia taught me an important lesson about bouncing back when things don't go my way. Everyone playing sport needs this skill and it has been valuable to me throughout my life.

Chris Robshaw

England and Harlequins rugby union captain.
Diagnosis meant his teachers could help him.
He resented the extra work at the time but it has
brought confidence and opportunities.

I don't think it was a shock when I first went to school and
didn't keep up. It was always the case that I wasn't up to speed
with the other guys. I had to work harder to do things others
found straightforward.

I was better at doing other things. I think a child always
needs something on which to anchor his confidence, and sport
was very much that for me. I was confident in the field, which
was very helpful for me in all ways. A lot of dyslexic people
have that – we are good at different sports or have a different
avenue to go down. We have something else.

Because I was dyslexic I probably worked harder at what
I did well, which was playing rugby. I found it very satisfying

and enjoyed getting praise for doing it as I didn't get so much praise in the classroom.

I was diagnosed quite young, I think at nine, and I had to do extra classes at school. Because the dyslexia was identified, my mum decided to send me to a boarding school, Millfield, that was very good for dyslexia. I was about 11 or 12 and it did feel young to be on the other side of the country.

I both liked being at boarding school and struggled with it. Of course I enjoyed being with my friends the whole time but I was also homesick at that age. My father had died when I was younger and it must have been tough for my mother to afford to send me to Millfield and also hard for her to send me away.

Millfield really helped me deal with the dyslexia. They gave me extra lessons in which the teachers were breaking subjects down so they were easier to understand. They had a different way of explaining things which was not conventional but which worked for me. The classes there were small – there were only about 12 of us in each – which must have made things easier. There were several other people with dyslexia there as well and I was never picked on by the others.

I'm sure catching the dyslexia early meant that the teachers had longer to deal with it and more could be done to help. They made me go to extra English classes, which at the time I hated. It felt like everyone else was outside playing and

I had to stay in and do all this extra work. Now, looking back, I am very glad they made me do this and it gave me a lot of confidence and brought me opportunities.

Everyone has tough experiences in life and tough things to overcome and dyslexia is just one of those. At least a lot of people with dyslexia have competencies elsewhere. There are lots of sportspeople, artists, musicians and others who have that creative side.

There are no major effects for me now. I'm a bit slow when it comes to reading and I only get through a couple of books a year. Because of this, I watch a fair bit of TV and I take in a lot of information in that way. My spelling's not as good as most, but it's not too bad. Luckily I'm not in an environment where writing is scrutinised so maybe this is less of an issue than for people with other jobs. If I hadn't succeeded in rugby I don't think I would have been in an office environment. I never have to take notes from a lecture or anything like that. If I'm in a meeting and have to remember what's being said I do take notes down then.

I think I am a visual person. If I see something I find it much easier to remember than I would something that was said to me. I often create a picture in my mind to help me remember something.

On the pitch you have to remember moves but, because you're on the pitch doing it, this somehow makes it easier. Before and during a game I have to remember line-up structures and patterns but the team usually has them drawn out on a board and then we go out and practise them. For me, as a visual person, this makes it much easier to take in than if someone just described them to me verbally.

When I was first at Harlequins my coach at Harlequin Academy played us a video and asked us what each position should do on the pitch at different times during the game. This broadened our view and knowledge of the game, again in a visual way, and meant that when we played we weren't only thinking about what we were doing in the game but what the whole team was doing.

I know life can be tough for children with dyslexia. As a kid you don't always see the bigger picture. My advice is always to make sure you enjoy what you do and work hard at it. Stick with it and try to learn. Really explore an avenue that you do enjoy and try to push it.

At school and in life you want to win everything all the time and sometimes you can't. Having dyslexia taught me an important lesson about bouncing back when things don't go my way. Everyone playing sport needs this skill and it has been valuable to me throughout my life. There are a lot of tough times in rugby as in any other job but it was my childhood dream to play for England and being England captain is a huge privilege and way beyond that dream. I have grabbed the opportunity with both hands.

I learned early on that, when people said
something was impossible, I shouldn't believe
them. This made me a trier and I am still trying.

Richard Rogers

Award-winning architect, well-known for his work on the Pompidou Centre in Paris, and the Lloyd's Building and Millennium Dome in London, and as an advisor on urban renaissance to mayors and governments across the world. His parents left Italy on the eve of the Second World War when he was a small child. His arrival at school in England was a shock.

For most of my school days, my ambition was to be second bottom of the class. No one had heard of dyslexia when I was young. I was just a 'stupid kid'. I didn't learn to read until I was 11, and that does knock your confidence. I was put into a separate group and labelled as incompetent and incapable of thinking, when I was just different.

My father was a doctor and was working full time. My mother was looking after me, but she caught TB and was sent away for two years to get healthy. I then went to boarding school, which I hated from the moment I arrived. I was beaten regularly and cried every night. I had no one to talk to or relate to. I had just come to the UK from Italy and only spoke a few words of English. We were at war with Italy, which gave the other children a reason to pick on me. I did make friends, but every day I had to do extra work because I couldn't keep up.

At seven or eight I was so desperate I considered jumping off a ledge. For a period, I completely lost my confidence. My wife Ruthie, who runs the River Cafe, says that when people come in to eat she doesn't notice if they might have a double first from Oxford. What she can tell is if people have had the confidence beaten out of them. She can see that almost immediately. It took me some years to get my confidence back.

Then I was sent to a school for children who had been defeated by the education system – I used to annoy my parents by calling it a 'school for backward children'. This was tremendous because I leapt from being not very good at school to being among the best! I did learn there but, when I was sent back to private school, I slipped back and had difficulties again.

The best thing about my life then was that I had the right parents. If you have dyslexia you need people to bolster you. My parents gave me love, support and a sense to aim upwards. Always up. This is the most important thing a parent can do – and it's free. I learned early on that, when people said something was impossible, I shouldn't believe them. This made me a trier and I am still trying.

A very large amount of what I learned was from extra lessons from my mother and father. I was fortunate that my mother stood by me when everyone said I should give up. At 16 I saw a specialist careers person who said I should stop all education, join the police and go to South Africa. I was a good boxer at the time, so my interpretation of this was that he was saying I should go there to 'hit the blacks round the ears'. Appalling.

After school and my National Service in Italy, someone realised I had a talent for design. I had developed a confidence, so I managed to talk my way into the Architectural Association (AA) School of Architecture – where I carried on failing. One of the lecturers wrote on my report, 'He has a genuine interest in and feeling for architecture but sorely lacks the intellectual equipment to translate these feelings into sound buildings.' But in the final year another lecturer, Peter Smithson, understood how I worked and I won the Year Prize. He realised there was more to me than what had been seen in my bad drawings.

This led to me going to study at Yale in the United States, having won a scholarship. I worked hard there – they do crazy hours – and the professors changed the direction of my architecture. I'm not good material for traditional, writing-based education, though I have strong visual awareness. I learned much more from travelling around the States, looking at the different buildings, seeing everything by Frank Lloyd Wright, the industrial heritage, the lightweight industrial construction of the Californian 'case study houses', the light and shadow. I realised the way forward was not to copy the masters, but to learn from them and to find a way to design buildings that interested me.

Before going to Yale, I worked in the architects' department at Middlesex County Council, but when I came back from the States, I formed Team 4, in partnership with my first wife Su, Norman Foster and his future wife Wendy Cheesman. The first houses we designed had all sorts of problems. I remember at the time despairing about whether I would ever make it as an architect. We all have crises, but you have to work through them. I don't really accept no's.

I am in my eighties and still work pretty hard. I could have retired years ago but, apart from family, there is nothing I enjoy more than work.

It is wonderful having won the RIBA gold medal, the Pritzker Prize and other awards, but I don't build for prizes or for straightforward acclaim. When Renzo Piano and I designed the Pompidou Centre in Paris, my wife Ruthie said, 'Don't read the bad articles,' and I said to her, 'There's nothing to read then.' The newspapers were negative but, when the Pompidou Centre opened and people started to come along and enjoy it, the press talked about it as if they had loved it all along. You need to find a way of not letting other people's views affect you, apart from the people who are important to you. Maybe I learned that as a schoolboy with dyslexia.

I didn't know that I had dyslexia until my kids were having trouble and people said to me, 'They've got dyslexia,' and I said, 'What the hell's that?' Dyslexia affects my memory and I have occasional word blindness. Even today I can't remember anyone's name. There are lots of jokes about it. The standard joke with Ruthie, who I am very much in love with, is that when we go to parties arm in arm, people say, 'Oh how nice that they are so close,' and Ruthie says, 'Actually, I'm here to whisper names to him.'

I am a life peer in the House of Lords, and when I am there I feel I can't greet people because of my problem with remembering names. It creates a particular kind of isolation. It is extremely difficult if you are talking to someone you know really well and can't remember their name.

Dyslexia also means that you have to put in more hours to get to the same place. I know I have to do more. I have to prepare well in advance for my talks.

Some people now think dyslexia is an attribute. Our minds do work in different ways. Having dyslexia makes you more able in some ways and less able in others. It probably does give you a certain visual sense. There is another argument that says because you are good at one area you develop that area, which meant I was less likely to be a lawyer and more likely to be an architect. So I think dyslexia may have helped me to be an architect but also I did love to do what I was good at; something to give me higher marks.

I have had wonderful colleagues throughout my life, wonderful people at work, wonderful support systems. I have just been lucky: architecture is my field and I was fortunate to find it. I believe building well civilises us. We have created a unique structure here at work. The company is owned by a charity. This allows us to share our good fortune with others. Greed is a terrible thing and it's very prevalent. Justice and fairness are very important to me.

Dyslexia also underlines our weaknesses, so teamwork is vital. I have a very good personal assistant who looks after me and can read my writing which is illegible and my spelling which is terrible. If we are lucky in our lives, we shape some of the world around us to make up for our difficulties – and our abilities can enhance the lives of people who may not have them.

If you have dyslexia and it's not recognised it is an appalling situation and you must fight for recognition and support. What we know about education and the working of the mind in general is still fragmented and partial. It is like the story of trying to describe an elephant, when you know where the tail is, where the trunk is and probably one ear – and that's as far as we've got. We only know bits and pieces, but that's what we have to work with. You have to learn all you can about the condition and to deal with it as a mother, father, child or teacher.

If you've already got something you're good at, like art or photography, then hook on to it; bolster your strengths. It's fascinating how people can adapt. Jewish people arrived in the States as tinker, tailor, soldier and sailor. That first generation heeled horses. The next generation are doctors and lawyers. People coming here from abroad with start-up companies do better than people who are already here. They have already made the big decision to leave wherever they were and they have that drive to make it here. It's about aiming high and, as people with dyslexia, that's what we do.

I know I was trying harder because of
having been a failure. I didn't want to be
a failure again. I looked for ways to take
advantage of the competition and do things
a little differently from everyone else.

Sir Jackie Stewart OBE

Three times Formula One motor-racing world champion **and** a champion shooter; now a businessman and President of Dyslexia Scotland. Semi-reclusive and desperate as a child while failing at school, he left at 15 to begin his motor career – washing windows and fixing tyres at his father's garage – determined never to fail again.

We got married when Helen was 21 and I was 23. For our first 19 years as husband and wife she didn't know that I couldn't read, spell or write. I was embarrassed to tell her and good at hiding it. I had won three world championships in motor racing, represented Great Britain at shooting and become a millionaire – and I still couldn't tell her the truth.

Keeping the secret wasn't as difficult as it might have been. My wife was the one who did the household accounts and helped our sons with their homework. I had a secretary to do my airline and hotel reservations and any letters that had to be written. I always managed to get others to do the things I couldn't.

I travelled a great deal as a racing driver and on every flight I was on, in every hotel I stayed in and every city I visited, I sent a postcard home to my sons when they were at school. I wrote the very same simple message which I had chosen carefully. 'I am on a plane. I am going to Washington/Sydney/Glasgow.' Some of the writing wasn't that good but that didn't matter. They were getting something with a stamp on it and a photograph on one side from a foreign country.

When I was 42, my son went for a dyslexia assessment and I was asked if I wanted to be tested as well. After this I finally said to Helen, 'I've just been told I'm dyslexic. I can't read or write properly.' She said to me, 'You can read and write,' and I said, 'No, I can't.'

It was an enormous relief to me when she found out. It was like being saved from drowning. We didn't argue about me not having told her. She was just amazed and she's still amazed about it now, more than 30 years later.

From the very beginning, school was a real disaster for me. The primary teacher was not sympathetic. Her job gave her the opportunity to show her teeth to those of us who I now realise were dyslexic.

At nine I was asked to recite a paragraph from a book in front of the class and I couldn't do it because all I could see was a jumble of words. The kids around me, 54 to a class, were coughing and spluttering and laughing. I felt humiliated.

This didn't only happen in class. Your gut is torn apart by having your inabilities shown up in front of everybody there, and then this moves from the classroom to the playground so I was isolated there too. Children are cruel and the clever ones would be abusing me and this gave me a huge complex. I was told I was dumb and so I believed it – and so would you if you were told you were dumb at a young age.

I had more 'illnesses' than you can count to try to avoid going into school. I kept making excuses for my bad school reports. My parents didn't know about dyslexia. Today people know more about it, and they still know precious little now.

My parents bought me time with a teacher at night to try to get me through the 11-plus exam and I used to distract him from the things I couldn't do. Dyslexics are good at learning how to duck and dive.

I failed my 11-plus twice. I remember that if you got an A in it you went on to do Latin and French, a B meant you did only French, a C you would get woodwork and a D woodwork and metalwork, cutting out a lot of the academic work. I scored a D and felt humiliated by that too.

Secondary school was as bad. I hated having to be sent to a different school from my friends. I remember lying awake at night, unable to sleep in my unhappiness.

These days I know kids sometimes turn to alcohol and drugs to escape the humiliation and the reality of their inabilities. I became semi-reclusive. I never joined the Cubs or Scouts or a church organisation for young people because I was frightened I might show myself up in a negative way. If you are humiliated in class and the playground, then you don't make friends. I hung out with the 'dummies', if you like, in other words the other boys with learning difficulties, in the bad part of town. When I was 14 I left there to go back home on the bus and I got attacked for no reason at all. Five boys all set upon me and left me with a broken collarbone, broken nose and three ribs cracked. I didn't even know who they were. This showed me I was in with the wrong people.

What saved me and saved my life was shooting. I started at 14 and won a trophy at the first event I entered even though I was competing against adults. This felt like the first time I was identifiably good at something by myself. While still a teenager I shot for Scotland and Great Britain, I went to the World Championships in Oslo and the European Championships in Geneva, Paris, Milan, Barcelona and Berne.

I left school at 15 with enormous relief and started work at the garage my father ran. I had a job serving petrol. I was polite to the customers and had great attention to detail. This meant I was very good at getting tips, which came to more than my wages. I kept the forecourt immaculate. Everything was spotless: the oil cabinets, petrol pumps and the office. I couldn't do the arithmetic, someone else did that, but I checked the batteries and tyres, fixed punctures and washed the windows. I was a perfectionist and, all these years on, my attention to detail is still my very best asset.

One of the customers offered me the chance to test a number of his cars and that's how I began my career in racing. I soon began to get noticed and started driving professionally. I know I was trying harder because of having been a failure. I didn't want to be a failure again. I looked for ways to take advantage of the competition and do things a little differently from everyone else.

I have a theory that the peripheral vision of some people with dyslexia is extra sharp. I would notice the first signs that the crowd at a race would begin to feel a few drops of rain. I would see an umbrella begin to go up in a grandstand of thousands of people! My hand–eye co-ordination is good too – vital for a Formula One driver or a trap shooter.

The racing car is like an animal. It recognises you doing things differently. It will tell if you're not as sensitive as you might be. I won most of my races in the first five laps. My head was clean, I was unemotional, focused. I didn't get over-excited. It would take me two to three days to get back to normal after a race, but it worked.

I knew I had to have the best mechanics because to finish first, first you must finish. If you haven't got good mechanics you will have mechanical failures. Again this is my attention to detail, the same on the track as it was in my father's garage. It meant my cars were more reliable. I won 27 Grands Prix from 99 starts. That's almost one in every three starts.

Still now I have really good staff to help me including a correspondence secretary, a diary and travel secretary and a personal assistant. I also have a theory that dyslexic people are more creative. All the clever folk think the same way but dyslexic people find other ways of doing the same thing. If everyone is driving on the M25 and it's overcrowded and bog slow, a dyslexic person will find the rural road with less traffic, less competition and they'll get there faster.

My son Mark is dyslexic and he has a boutique film production company. One of the films he has made is about the last man on the moon. Everyone knows who the first man on the moon was, but no one knows the last. That to me is typically dyslexic, thinking about things in a different way.

If you have dyslexia you have to try harder and you have to be more creative. Look at George Lucas – who else could have thought of **Star Wars**. Or Muhammad Ali, seeing the punch coming and avoiding being hit. Footballers looking for where the ball might come to and being there when it comes.

I still struggle with my reading and writing. I procrastinate if I am writing a thank-you letter. It takes me so long and so many attempts. I have to phone my secretary to ask how to spell something because I can't find it in the dictionary. I might send off the fifth attempt. It won't be right but hopefully they will know I am dyslexic. I can't use an iPod or an iPhone. I can receive messages from voicemail but not text messages. I don't have an iPad and can't find my own name on a keyboard.

I still can't recite the alphabet and I don't know the words of the Lord's Prayer or the National Anthem. Dyslexia never goes away, it's just that you find ways round it.

I have great sympathy for other people with dyslexia. My advice would always be to find something they are good at and do it well. If I had been a window cleaner I would have done it well. I could have been a world champion window cleaner! I'd have done it so well I would have cleaned your windows and you would have wanted me back. I couldn't have done all the streets so I would have employed another dyslexic. Soon there'd have been a bunch of us.

Look for the opportunities. Most people's garages are a mess. What if you went in and made their garage terrific, painted the floor and the walls, hung things on the wall so they weren't scattered on the floor. They would boast about their tidy garage to the neighbours and then the neighbours would want you to do theirs.

I get totally frustrated by Government and Westminster, dealing with Ministers of Education trying to get them to help more with dyslexia. Lord Adonis was great but then he was moved and was followed by others who were looking for ways of not doing things, but I did think Gove was good also. Things are different in Scotland, where the Scottish Government gave £1.4 million to get a seat created at the University of Aberdeen for learning disabilities. We then got all the deans of the teacher training colleges in Scotland to make sure that every new teacher has the skills and ability to recognise children with learning disabilities. This was approved when I got Scotland's First Minister at the time, Alex Salmond, to assemble the deans in his conference room with the then Minister of Education, the CEO of Dyslexia Scotland and myself, and implored them to create it. Outside of Scotland, few of the teacher training colleges in the UK have all of their students learning about early recognition of learning disabilities. At least ten per cent of the 5 million people in Scotland have problems with reading and writing – that's between 500,000 and 750,000 men and women, boys and girls. Surely something more needs to be done?

Of the prison population in Scotland, more than 70 per cent can't read or write, which means they usually can't get a job. They get unemployment benefit, which costs the country a fortune and doesn't pay as well as crime. So they go to jail. Now we are helping to teach people in jail to read and write and be computer literate. Most don't want to admit it so we don't get to them all but we do reach a lot of them.

By openly admitting my dyslexia I have been able to help others. Everyone has to have a chance in life. A policeman called me and said he was about to get the sack because he hadn't told his employers he was dyslexic and he couldn't do some of the paperwork. I explained the problem to the Chief Constable and we had a big meeting with other police forces to see what could be done to help people in his position.

So get your dyslexia recognised. If you're at school, ask the teachers to explain to the class that you have a dyslexia problem. When I speak at schools I always tell them I am considerably more successful than anyone else was in my 54-person school class. I say, 'You be nice to Fred. He's dyslexic and one day you might be working for him. Fred will find something he's good at and when he does he will be better than anyone.'

There are many people in the arts who are
dyslexic and who have many different forms
of dyslexia. It's extraordinary how many have
surmounted it without really knowing it. A focus
on the arts develops a vital muscle in the brain.

Zoë Wanamaker CBE

Award-winning stage, film and television actor, star of **Harry Potter**, Agatha Christie's **Poirot**, **Mr Selfridge**, **My Family** and many more. Learning lines has meant a great deal of extra work, but dyslexia also propels her to achieve.

I was officially diagnosed with dyslexia relatively recently, in 2004. Giving my problem a name was something of a relief and somehow I felt exonerated.

All my life I have struggled with retaining information. When I went to be tested for dyslexia I found that I could remember the first paragraph of what I was reading and after that the information became blurred. This is what seems to occur when learning lines. Sometimes I remember a sentence but then conjunctive words slide off into a void. Consequently I sit with a script for a very long time.

How this affects me at work depends on the part I am playing. Learning the script for **Stevie**, the play about the poet and novelist Stevie Smith, was a recent challenge because a lot of it is seemingly monologue. Rehearsals started in March and I began learning the script four months earlier. By January I realised I needed outside help and I found someone to read with me and correct me. It is a painstaking job.

Another hurdle is learning lines with a foreign accent – needing to achieve the accuracy of the script plus the accuracy of the tone.

Theatre and television are completely different animals. The turnover of scripts is far speedier with television and something like a situation comedy, for example **My Family**, highlights the problem.

A new script would arrive on a Friday and there would be a read-through and rehearsals would start. Then on Monday there would be rewrites and on Wednesday we would pre-record the scenes which couldn't technically be performed in front of an audience. On Thursday, along with the dress rehearsal, the whole script was shot and filmed in front of an audience and then a new script would come on Friday and the whole process would start again.

Consequently I was confronted with having to learn a new script every week, which made me feel under enormous pressure. At times I felt the dialogue was lacking in imagination or rhythm; sentences short and sometimes inconsequential, sometimes out of character. Dialogue is easier to learn when it's well written. For example I find Shakespeare with his innate rhythm relatively easy to learn. Because it is iambic it is in our DNA.

The job of any creative human being is to make it look effortless. An audience should never be aware of your insecurities. For me, it is cripplingly humiliating not to know my lines and to go wrong in front of an audience in any situation.

I want to know the lines so well that they are soaked into the sponge that is my brain and I don't have to feel anxious about them. You can screw up once and the audience will love it when you make a mistake but do it twice and it's not so comfortable and then I beat myself up. Sometimes I had lines written on my wrist or on a chopping board in the kitchen on set, or on any bits of furniture the audience didn't see.

I began to sit down with the stage managers after rehearsals and stay behind for a couple of hours and work with them every day of the week to make sure the dialogue went into my head. I also went to a hypnotherapist, which helped to some extent.

The younger you are the quicker it is to learn, the older you are the more difficult it becomes. The fear for every performer is not being able to remember your script. This is terrifying because you lose your income, your dignity and – most importantly – your self-belief, which is the most fragile thing for everybody. Self-belief is a candle that's easy to blow out and difficult to relight. It's all about the fear of failure.

I became an actress and went into the theatre after studying at drama school for three years. Before this I was lucky enough to go to a progressive, co-educational school where the class sizes were around 20. I had this privileged upbringing but my brain still wouldn't engage when I tried to retain facts.

In class I was always somewhere else, looking out of the window. When I was 12 they said, 'Forget maths, you don't have to worry about that,' which was a great relief. An iron door comes down in my brain when numbers are mentioned.

I was miserable at school and felt I had no right to be. My parents had worked hard and spent a lot of money on my private education and I was screwing up and must have been a disappointment. My father always told me I had the attention of a flea and my mother was worried about me. I think the teachers saw me as another creature. I couldn't understand English grammar and still don't. There's always a bully and I had one at one point. The arts were all that interested me but when it came to the academic side I was away with the pixies. I went to another school to do my exams but by then it was too late.

Art school was a revelation and when at drama school I was never late. For the first time I was excited about what I was learning.

Dyslexia has made me want to achieve more in what I am good at, but I also know my limitations in a much healthier way. However, like many people, I will do the gardening or the cleaning or anything rather than sit down and look at the text I am meant to be learning (which to me is like doing homework).

I have to be sure of a subject to be able to sell it, which is why learning lines and knowing characters and knowing why and what and where and how is imperative. It is knowledge and a structure that give me confidence in what I'm doing.

When researching a character, ironically I do a lot of reading. I've learned more about history, sociology and the human psyche because they give context to my work. I've always been very visual. I look at a lot of pictorial imagery and photography. I also listen to the music of the period.

Costume is very important, extremely helpful. All of this builds up a character.

Put it all together and it becomes a piece of art, something creative, and it gives me confidence that I can see who she is and what her life is like, whatever the character.

There are many people in the arts who are dyslexic and who have many different forms of dyslexia. It's extraordinary how many people have surmounted it without really knowing it. A focus on the arts develops a vital muscle in the brain.

I became a patron of a school which specialises in working with children with dyslexia. At a prize-giving there a young man, an ex-pupil, spoke. He was a pilot. He gave this wonderful speech about how he was told he could never be a pilot and he now flies for British Airways. That summer on holiday I met a young boy who was at another school for dyslexic students and desperately wanted to fly. His parents were very concerned about it but I told him about this extraordinary speech I'd heard and told him, 'You have to do it.' Eighteen months later I heard that he had flown solo. I have a photograph to prove it.

The staff at Dyslexia Action who tested me for dyslexia advised me to think not that, 'I am dyslexic,' but that, 'I have dyslexia.' I think it's a wonderful thing that if you accept dyslexia and what it means for you, it can make you very determined. It won't stop you.

Perhaps because I have had difficulties it is very easy to have empathy for people who are going through hard times, and people do go through far, far worse. It is a huge privilege that people trust me enough to write to me in intimate detail.

Zelda West-Meads

Highly respected 'agony aunt' for the **Mail on Sunday's You** magazine, counsellor and former spokesperson for Relate. Found not being able to read or spell like the other girls at school highly painful, though her teachers and parents never doubted her intelligence.

As a child I didn't achieve and I didn't know why. It was devastating. I felt that I must be stupid but I knew inside that I wasn't. Of course this had a huge effect on my self-esteem. I am a very driven person, quite ambitious and have a career I love, yet even now I am one of those people who think that they will be 'found out', because of the damage done to me as a child through not knowing that I was dyslexic.

When I was at school I hadn't even heard of the word dyslexia. I don't know if anyone had. But I minded hugely that the standard of my work was different. I had to move schools seven times as a child because my father, an incredibly bright man, was a naval officer and kept being posted to different places. Every time I was interviewed for a new school, I would do well and was often put in a group with girls a year older than myself. Then when I started and they found that I couldn't write, spell and read like the others, they wanted to move me down, which was a huge shock.

I think perhaps the worst thing for dyslexic children is to have to stand up, read out loud and be compared with their peer group. When I was 12 and at a school in Malta, there was an English master who would stand behind me and every time I got a word wrong – which was every other word – he hit me so hard that it hurt, on the shoulder and on the head. I remember some children laughing and my fear of reading out loud became worse. My parents did, after a while, send me to another school. I also remember teachers making fun of me because I couldn't spell, drawing even more attention to me when it was bad enough that I had noticed it myself.

When they pinned our exam results up on the board, I wanted to start looking at the top to see how I'd done but I had to start looking at the bottom where my name was usually first. I found that very embarrassing, upsetting and confusing; perhaps confusing more than anything. I thought, 'Why can't I do this? I don't understand…'

If only I had known at seven that I was dyslexic, it would have made a huge difference. It's so important for young people that dyslexia is diagnosed early, so they are not confused when things that seem relatively easy to others are hard for them. Life is difficult as a child with dyslexia, particularly when it is not recognised. It's a hurdle to climb over.

Teachers should be very sensitive to dyslexic children because other children can be unkind. I remember some children being cruel but I also had very good friends, which helped.

My parents were supportive too. My mother was an intelligent woman and spoke five languages. Even when I was struggling, I knew my parents never doubted my intelligence. I talked to my mother who didn't understand why I wasn't doing better because she could see I was a bright little girl. They tried to encourage me to read and I taught myself with books at home. They weren't pushy parents; they just wanted me to do as well as I could and enjoy school. I was an only child and mature for my age, mixing mainly with adults, so I think that they felt that my maturity compensated for my results.

Also, because I moved schools so often, I learned how to survive and fit in with other people. I learned the value of friendship because my problems with learning meant life was quite difficult and I valued and understood others at an early age. All of this was very useful to me in life and in my work.

The other schools I went to were a lot better than that one in Malta, apart from the occasional teacher. I left school at 15 with a single O-level in RE (all my other exams were unmarked because they couldn't read my handwriting) because my father was being posted to Hong Kong. Believe it or not I got a job teaching English and History to Chinese children. I took my dictionary everywhere.

I came back to this country at 16 when my parents got divorced. I would love to have gone to university but couldn't. I worked for a couple of years pushing paper around in envelopes, which was pretty soul-destroying, and then another running an office. I also did some modelling between jobs. Because of the divorce, there was no money to pay for any training.

I didn't realise that I was dyslexic until my mid-twenties when I applied to the National Marriage Guidance Council, which is now Relate. I had married young, at 21, and had a son and a daughter very quickly. When they started school I saw an advert for becoming a counsellor. I have always loved and been interested in people, and friends often talked to me about their problems. It offered free training and it sounded interesting so I applied.

The selection for the training was at a centre in Rugby and it was going very well until I discovered that we had to do a written exam. I thought, 'Well this is it. No chance.' Then the psychiatrist who was doing the interviews called me in individually. I was worried. He had my test paper in front of him and instead of telling me that I hadn't made the grade, as I expected, he said, 'Do you know you are actually severely dyslexic?'

This was the first time I had heard this. Even now, when I remember that moment I feel tearful because suddenly everything I had been struggling with made sense. I was accepted as a trainee counsellor and this was the start of a career that I loved and still love.

We had very little money when the children were young. The counselling was voluntary but if you worked more than a certain number of hours you were paid a little so I worked pretty much all the time during school hours.

My local Marriage Guidance organisation wanted to buy its own premises. No one wanted to fundraise so I offered to do the job and I raised the money in a year. As a result, I was asked to go and work at the national headquarters and continued working as a fundraiser, including raising my own salary.

While working at head office I also realised that no one was doing any media work. If a journalist rang, all the telephones would ring, in one office after another, because no one wanted to take the call. I suggested that I could be their press officer and they said, 'Okay, but you still have to raise your own salary!' So I did the fundraising and PR.

Of course PR meant a lot of writing. Ironically, in spite of my problems, I had always wanted to be a writer. In fact, as a little girl with dyslexia I thought, 'I will have to marry a writer because I can't write myself.' But press releases are only short and by then I had a secretary so I could dictate them. It turned out that I must have had a flair for publicity. My press releases always got a huge amount of coverage, not necessarily because of the quality of my work but because for the first time people were writing about relationships. And I was able to write anything I liked because no one else at Marriage Guidance knew anything about PR so I could be quite controversial.

I was invited to do lots of radio and TV interviews and I always did a huge amount of preparation beforehand, probably because of the insecurity of childhood.

Eventually, a publisher approached me and asked me to write three self-help books. At one stage, this would have seemed impossible but by then I had done a lot of writing for my career so I was more used to it. Also, I had learned so much through counselling that it didn't seem so hard to write about relationships. I had a wonderful editor, Rowena Webb, at Hodder & Stoughton. Heaven knows what she thought of my grammar and punctuation, but she never said a word about it. Each book took me a whole year to write.

My daughter Caroline who is, ironically, an editor is less reticent about my grammar and spelling mistakes. At around the same time as I was writing the books, **You** magazine, the **Mail on Sunday's** supplement, asked me to apply to be its agony aunt. Caroline has edited pretty much every column I have ever written prior to sending it in to the magazine and she will ring me up and laugh saying, 'Can you really not tell the difference between prostate and protest?' I will have put a word through the spellchecker but got the original spelling so wrong that it has put in a correctly spelled word but completely in the wrong context. She despairs at what she calls my 'complete lack of punctuation' and sends me wonderfully funny e-mails about the difference it makes. I love my children beyond anything so I don't mind taking the criticism. She does it so sweetly anyway.

I know there's nothing wrong with my thought processes. It's actually being able to put my thoughts down on paper, which is where the blockage is. In fact my thoughts come very fast, much faster than I am able to type, but then I look down at what I've written and think, 'What does **that** say?'

Without a doubt, my work takes me longer than it would if I wasn't dyslexic. I can read easily enough now because, perhaps unusually for a dyslexic, I actually love reading. I always have a novel on the go and I love poetry. But I am not a quick reader. If my readers' letters are handwritten, it is harder and I can't always tell every word. Luckily most are e-mailed now, which I find easier. Some of the letters I get however are six or seven pages long: 'I'll start in 1960…' In some ways, this is helpful as you get a much fuller idea of a person's life and more understanding of their problem, but of course they also take me ages to read.

It's not easy cutting seven pages to the small amount of space that I have for each letter and answer. Sometimes there are such moving details and so much information but I just have to leave it out. That's just how magazines are.

Sometimes I am able to reply personally to people whose letters I haven't been able to include on the page. My daughter doesn't check these letters and I do wonder what people think of me when they see my spelling. So I would like to apologise to them now! What is lovely is that I get fantastic letters back, some saying, 'You've made a real difference to my life. You're the only person I've been able to tell about this.'

I really love trying to help people. I still work privately as a counsellor as well. Perhaps because I have had difficulties it is very easy to have empathy for people who are going through hard times, and people do go through far, far worse. It is a huge privilege that people trust me enough to write to me in intimate detail.

For children with dyslexia, I think the most important thing I'd say to them is to make sure you value yourselves and realise that being dyslexic doesn't make you in any way less than anyone else. It can make life much harder at school (though of course there is much more help and understanding these days) but, although you have to work harder, it can make you even more determined to succeed. A lot of dyslexic children are in fact extremely intelligent and many dyslexics have been very successful as adults.

If some of the children tease you then talk to your friends, family or teachers. The ones being unkind are really not worth it. Take the extra time you're given in exams and really believe in yourself. You're not stupid and there is nothing to stop you being just as successful as anyone else.

For parents, it's vital to believe in your child and make sure they get the help they need, even if you have to fight for it within the school. You're doing it for your child so there couldn't be a more important cause to fight for. Give your child lots of reassurance so they never feel they are less good than anyone else. Dyslexia can affect self-esteem, as I know only too well.

Some schools pride themselves on being very academic so the pressure these days is quite a concern. I get a lot of letters from teenagers and I'm sure there is an increase in self-harming, anorexia and bulimia. Often children have problems and parents can be too preoccupied to notice, even if they are loving people.

I was very concerned that my children wouldn't have the struggles I had and I taught them both to read and write before they went to school. Though my son never liked writing and still doesn't, he was an avid reader and when he was little I would often find him at midnight with a torch under the bedclothes, desperate to finish his **Famous Five** book before the morning.

I was hugely relieved that my children weren't dyslexic but one of my grand-daughters is. She's very clever too but I know that she finds it frustrating. She says lots of girls at her school are dyslexic.

Dyslexia is a very tough lesson but it drove me to achieve. I always felt that I had something to prove. It taught me to compete, not with others but with myself. I know it helps my grand-daughter to see what I do. I hope it helps her to know that you can be dyslexic and still be successful.

We are the creative people. Use it to your
advantage. See the world differently.
Us dyslexic people, we've got it going on – we
are the architects. We are the designers.

Benjamin Zephaniah

Describes himself as a 'poet, writer, lyricist, musician and troublemaker'. Was thrown out of school at 13, had run-ins with the police but made a series of decisions to turn his life around.

In many ways being dyslexic is a natural way to be. What's unnatural is the way we read and write.

If you look at a pictorial language like Chinese, you can see the word for a woman because the character looks like a woman. The word for a house looks like a house. Early languages were like that. It is a strange step to go from that to a squiggle that represents a sound, which is how we read and write here.

If you're dyslexic and you feel there's something holding you back, just remember: it's not you. It's the way things at school or in society are presented to you. If someone can't understand dyslexia it's their problem, not yours. In the same way, if someone oppresses me because of my race I don't sit down and think, 'How can I become white?' It's not my problem, it's theirs and they have to come to terms with it.

So, if you are dyslexic, don't be heavy on yourself. And if you are a parent of someone with dyslexia don't think of it as a deformity. You may have a genius on your hands! I think having dyslexia can make you creative. If you want to construct a sentence and can't find the word you are searching for, you have to think of a way to write round it. This is being creative and your 'creativity muscle' gets bigger. That's the way architects work. They see a problem, maybe a building has to be taller or has to keep the light out, and find a way to deal with it. They don't just come across a problem, go to a text book and find out what it says. In fact I've come to the conclusion that dyslexia is the human race's default position. I presume everyone's dyslexic and wait for people to tell me they're not!

There is a high percentage of the prison population who are dyslexic, and a high percentage of the architect population as well. If you look at the book of statistics, I should be in prison: a black man brought up on the wrong side of town whose family fell apart, in trouble with the police when I was a kid, unable to read and write, with no qualifications and on top of that dyslexic. But I think staying out of prison is about conquering your fears and finding your path in life.

When I go into prisons to talk to people I see men and women who, in terms of their intelligence and their other qualities, are the same as me. But we reached a point in life where I went in one direction and they went in another.

Opportunities opened for me and they missed theirs, didn't notice them or didn't take them.

What helped me make the right choices was being observant. When I was in borstal (what they used to call a young person's prison) I used to do this thing of looking at people I didn't want to be like. I saw this guy who was there with me who spent all his time sitting stooped over and I thought, 'I don't want to be like that,' so I learned to sit with a straight back. I met a girl recently who told me she wanted to give up studying to have a good time and I told her to look at the people on the streets near where she was living – the payday loaners, the gamblers, the bookies, the red light areas – and tell herself she didn't want to live like them. Invest now and have a good time later. I just heard from her and she's made it to St Andrew's University.

Dyslexia is a weird word for the inability to spell and read. It is a difficult word. Most people now grow up with the word but when someone first told me I had dyslexia it sounded as if they were saying I had some kind of disease.

This happened when I was 21 when I went to an adult education class in London to learn to read and write. As I started to learn, the teacher said, 'You are dyslexic,' and I was like, 'Do I need an operation?'

She explained to me what it meant and I suddenly thought, 'Ah, I get it. I thought I was going crazy.' Having a word for it was great.

I had just published my first book so I already had the confidence that I wasn't stupid. I had told my poems to my girlfriend who had written them down for me. My mantra was then – and still is now – that dyslexia is not a measure of my or anyone else's intelligence. People were reading about my book and talking about it, especially within the black community. It had really taken off. I now knew I had this thing called dyslexia and it hadn't stopped me from being a poet.

People still ask me how I can be a writer and dyslexic but I always tell them it's easy. A machine printed the book, not me. You're not buying the book for my handwriting but for my ideas. Getting the ideas in there is a process called writing but I can find a way round that to get my stuff on paper.

When I was really coming up as a writer I had to write things down and didn't know I was dyslexic so I didn't know there was anything to fight against. I wrote a lot of my poems phonetically: 'wid luv' for 'with love'. People didn't think they were dyslexic poems, they just thought I wrote phonetically.

Still now, when I'm writing the word 'knot', I have to stop and think, 'How do I write that?' I'm thinking for ages about the word. I have to draw something to let me know what the word is to come back to it later. If I can't spell 'question' I just put a question mark and come back to it later. If I can't spell a name I don't avoid it. I use it in a novel I'm writing, which makes me learn it.

I'm of the generation where you went to school and teachers didn't know what dyslexia was. They weren't trained to know about it. The big problem with the education system then was that there was no compassion, no understanding and no humanity. There was no consideration for people who were different.

I don't look back and feel angry with the teachers. The ones who wanted to be creative and have an individual approach to their students weren't allowed to anyway. The idea of being kind and thoughtful and listening to problems just wasn't done. The past is a different kind of country, really.

It's a sad thing to say but no one gave me any encouragement at school, besides one sports teacher because I was a really fast runner. No one ever said to me, 'You've got some good ideas.' For my ideas I was always told to shut up.

My ideas always contradicted the teachers' ideas. I remember once a teacher saying that human beings sleep for one third of their life and I put my hand up and said, 'If there's a God isn't that a design fault? If you've built something, you want efficiency. You want it to be running most of the time. If I was God I would have designed sleep so we could stay awake. Then good people could do one third more good in the world.'

The teacher said, 'Shut up, stupid boy. Bad people would do one third more bad.' I thought I'd put in a good idea. I was just being creative. She also had a point, but the thing was she called me stupid for even thinking about it.

I remember a teacher talking about Africa and the 'local savages' and I would say, 'Who are you to talk about savages?' She would say, 'How dare you challenge me,' and that would get me into trouble. Deep down I knew teachers can't be right all of the time, and that my ideas had some merit. After class some of the other kids would say to me, 'You were right. Why did she put you down like that?'

If there's something going on in front of class and kids aren't connected with it, they stare out of the window. Or they start having a conversation or pass things between them. That's just what you do. Once, when I was finding it difficult to engage with writing and had asked for some help, a teacher said, 'It's all right. We can't all be intelligent, but you'll end up being a good sportsperson so why don't you go outside and play some football?' I thought, 'Oh great', and the other kids were looking at me really jealous, the boys especially. Now I realise he was stereotyping me.

I had poems in my head even then and when I was 10 or 11 my sister wrote some of them down for me. When I was 13 I could read very basically but it would be such hard work that I would give up. I knew other people were finding it easier but I didn't know anybody who was reading books. I thought that so long as you could read how much the banknote was worth and basic things like that you knew enough or you could ask a mate.

I got thrown out of a lot of schools, the last one at 13. I was expelled partly because of questioning and arguing with teachers on an intellectual level and partly for being a rude boy and fighting. I was really bad. I didn't stab anybody but I did take revenge on a teacher once. I stole his car and drove it into his front garden. He was a member of the racist organisation, the National Front, and I remember him telling us the Nazis weren't that bad, they got a bad press. He could say that in the classroom! Things are certainly better now, though they can always improve more.

When I was growing up, in Handsworth in Birmingham, there was no one about who was like the person I wanted to be. My dad was a postman and my mum was a nurse. I wanted to be a poet who was serious, political, on the radio, on television, in books. There was Muhammad Ali and what he stood for, but no black British role models so I had to create one.

I never thought I was stupid. I didn't have that struggle. In class they would call me stupid but inside I knew I wasn't. What happened happened, and I got kicked out of school but deep inside I knew I didn't have to spend the rest of my life in prison. Another of my mantras is that some of the most fascist, racist, sexist, terrible people in the world are not dyslexic – are they cleverer than you? If I have someone in front of me who doesn't have a problem reading and writing telling me that black people are savages I just think, 'Well who are you? I'm not stupid – you're the one who's stupid.' I just had this self-belief. There were no role models to inspire me; it was just something I knew. I remember this teacher implying I was a bit dumb and my life would go nowhere and I was already being paid £100 a night for a poetry gig. I thought, 'You're supposed to be teaching me this English language and I've got it and run with it.' It was ironic.

I was very self-motivated and became very 'successful' and then doors opened for me. I wrote more poetry, novels for teenagers, plays, other books and recorded music. I have 17 honorary doctorates! I take poetry to people who do not read poetry.

When Brunel University offered me the job of Professor of Poetry and Creative Writing I spent a year thinking about it, making sure it was for me and that I could see a purpose in it. I knew my students would be officially more educated than me and probably better read than me. I am here because of my experience. I tell my students, 'You can do this course and get the right grade because you have a good memory – but if you don't have passion, creativity, individuality, there's no point.'

In my life now, I find that people accommodate my dyslexia. I can perform my poetry in public because it doesn't have to be word perfect, but I never read one of my novels in public. When I go to literary festivals I always get an actor to read it out for me. If I do the reading all my energy goes to the book and I have lost the mood. My concentration is on getting all the words right, getting the inflection right and sometimes I start rewriting it and adding words in. That's why I don't do the reading myself. I can read from an autocue if I'm presenting a programme because it's okay then if I change a word or two.

I was just talking to a student with dyslexia like mine. She can read a page and realise she hasn't taken it in. Then she has to jump back and read it again. Then she reads it and puts her own words into it and that's what I do.

When I look at a book, the first thing I see is the size of it and I know that's what it's like for a lot of young people who find reading tough.

I struggle with filling in forms – I think most people with dyslexia struggle with that. I sometimes have to read them over and over again. Sometimes I say, 'This form needs to be posted by this date. I will read this paragraph and make sure I understand it. Then the next day I will read the next paragraph.' I fill it in a little bit at a time. Break things down. The most complicated forms I have are my contracts and my agent does them for me and talks to me about what they mean in reality.

When kids come up to me and say, 'Can I take your photograph? I'm dyslexic too,' which happens all the time, I tell them, 'We are the creative people. Use it to your advantage. See the world differently. Us dyslexic people, we've got it going on – we are the architects. We are the designers.' It's like they are proud of me and if that helps them, that is great. I didn't have that. I always say to them, 'Bloody non-dyslexics…who do they think they are?'

About Dyslexia

- Dyslexia primarily affects the ability to learn to read and spell.

- It comes from a difficulty in dealing with the sounds of words, which makes it especially hard to learn to read words using phonics.

- It usually affects short-term memory and speed of recalling names or labels. This means that people with dyslexia often find it hard to remember lists of things they have just heard, or to remember a name or a fact quickly.

- Other kinds of difficulties, for example difficulties with maths or with co-ordination, may go alongside dyslexia, but they do not always, and they are not part of the definition.

- Dyslexia is not the same for everyone: it can be mild or severe; it varies depending on other strengths or difficulties that the person may have, and it varies depending on the kind of support and encouragement that is given at school, at home and at work.

Leading dyslexia charity Dyslexia Action says...

- People with dyslexia often have strengths in reasoning, in visual and creative fields; dyslexia is not related to general intelligence, and is not the result of visual difficulties.

- Dyslexia usually runs in families. Even though genes are involved, there is still much that can be done, especially if intervention is given early.

- Many people learn strategies to manage the effects of dyslexia, but it does not go away and its effects may be felt in new situations or in times of stress.

- People with dyslexia often, but not always, show characteristics of other specific learning difficulties such as dyspraxia, attention deficit disorder or dyscalculia.

Signs of dyslexia include...

- Slowness in learning to read, write and spell.

- Slow speed of writing, spelling and reading and/or needing to read something several times before it is understood.

- Continuing to make visual errors in reading, for example saying 'was' for 'saw' or 'bad' for 'dad'.

- Making 'bizarre' spelling errors that seem unrelated by sound to the intended word.

- Difficulties working out sums 'in the head', confusing or forgetting telephone numbers, and problems remembering instructions.

- Using the wrong name for something or problems saying long, complicated words like 'preliminary' and 'statistical'.

- Appearing forgetful or disorganised.

If you are concerned that your child has dyslexia...

Dyslexia Action recommends taking the following steps:

- Write a list of your concerns and the reasons why you feel your child may have dyslexia.

- Speak to your child's class teacher and/or head of year about your concerns. It may be recommended that an assessment is appropriate.

- Make an appointment with either Dyslexia Action or the Special Educational Needs Co-ordinator (SENCO) at your child's school to discuss the options available, or the possibility of an assessment from a Local Authority Psychologist.

- Discuss the assessment report with your child's teacher and/or the SENCO and set in place an action plan.

Where to Go for Help

Seeking help is vital for anyone who may have dyslexia.

UK
Dyslexia Action
www.dyslexiaaction.org.uk
Dyslexia Action House
10 High Street
Egham
Surrey
TW20 9EA
Tel: 0300 303 8357
e-mail: info@dyslexiaaction.org.uk

A national charity with over 40 years' experience in providing services and support to children, young people and adults with literacy and numeracy difficulties, dyslexia and other specific learning difficulties. It provides assessments and tuition through its national learning centres and in schools across the country. It supports teachers and educators through the provision of teaching resources and training. It also undertakes research and campaigning to improve the lives of those affected by dyslexia.

To find out where your nearest Dyslexia Action Learning Centre is located and for details of how to contact the Centre visit www.dyslexiaaction.org.uk

British Dyslexia Association
www.bdadyslexia.org.uk
Tel: 0333 405 4555
Helpline: 0333 405 4567
Helpline opening hours: Monday–Friday 10am–1pm and 1.30–4pm, except Wednesday 10am–1pm
e-mail via www.bdadyslexia.org.uk/contact

Resources and support for children and adults with dyslexia. The BDA aims to influence government and other institutions to promote a dyslexia-friendly society, that enables dyslexic people of all ages to reach their full potential.

It campaigns to encourage schools to work towards becoming dyslexia-friendly, to reduce the number of dyslexic young people in the criminal justice system and to enable dyslexic people to achieve their potential in the workplace.

Dyslexia Scotland
www.dyslexiascotland.org.uk
2nd floor – East Suite
Wallace House
17–21 Maxwell Place
Stirling
FK8 1JU
Tel: 01786 446650
Helpline: 0844 800 84 84

Helpline opening hours: Monday to Thursday 10am–4.30pm,
Friday 10am–4pm
e-mail: helpline@dyslexiascotland.org.uk

Encourages and enables people with dyslexia, regardless of
their age and abilities, to reach their potential. It provides
services, influences change at a national and local level, gives
dyslexic people a voice and supports a network of branches,
members and partners.

Dyslecsia Cymru / Wales Dyslexia

www.walesdyslexia.org.uk
For all enquiries please contact the Freephone bilingual
helpline with trained volunteers.
Tel: 0808 1800 110
Helpline opening hours: Monday 5–8pm, Wednesday 5–8pm,
Monday, Thursday or Friday mornings
e-mail: chair@walesdyslexia.org.uk

Offers advice and support to private individuals, third sector
organisations, public bodies and private businesses in Wales.

Northern Ireland Dyslexia Association

www.nida.org.uk
17a Upper Newtownards Road
Belfast
BT4 3HT
Tel: 028 9065 9212
e-mail: help@nida.org.uk

An organisation to help parents, teachers, other professionals
and dyslexic learners in Northern Ireland.

Helen Arkell Dyslexia Centre

www.arkellcentre.org.uk

Arkell Lane

Farnham

GU10 3BL

Tel: 01252 792400

e-mail: enquiries@arkellcentre.org.uk

Offers dyslexia assessment and dyslexia help from its centre in Surrey, covering the whole of the UK.

The Dyslexia Association

www.dyslexia.uk.net

Helpline: 0115 924 6888

Helpline opening hours: Monday–Friday 9.30am–4.30pm

Operates a confidential helpline for people with dyslexia of all ages, plus services in the East Midlands.

Dyslexics.org.uk

www.dyslexics.org.uk

An independent website with advice for parents and grandparents, primary teachers, SENCOs, tutors and others.

Dyslexia Research Trust

www.dyslexic.org.uk
Dyslexia Research Trust
The Sherrington Building
Department of Physiology Anatomy and Genetics
Parks Road
Oxford
OX1 3PT

Dyslexia Research Trust
179A Oxford Road
Reading
RG1 7UZ
Tel: 0118 958 5950
e-mail: info@dyslexic.org.uk

Oxford University based charity which investigates new and effective approaches to reading problems.

Adult Dyslexia Organisation

www.adult-dyslexia.org
e-mail via www.adult-dyslexia.org/content/contact or ado.
dns@dial.pipex.com

A UK organisation which provides a range of employment, educational, legal information and materials to meet the needs of dyslexic adults.

Dyslexia Help

www.dyslexiahelp.co.uk

Articles, tips and teaching ideas, and links to other useful sites for dyslexia teaching, assessment and resources.

Ireland

Dyslexia Association of Ireland

www.dyslexia.ie
5th Floor
Block B
Joyce's Court
Talbot Street
Dublin 1
Tel: 01 877 6001
e-mail: info@dyslexia.ie

Supporting children and adults with dyslexia in Ireland. Dyslexia Association of Ireland aims to promote the understanding, treatment and prevention of the problems which can be associated with dyslexia. The association lobbies for appropriate services for people with dyslexia, and acts as a service provider, offering assessment, specialist tuition, and training. It aims to increase awareness and understanding of dyslexia.

USA
International Dyslexia Association
www.interdys.org

40 York Road

4th Floor

Baltimore

MD 21204

Tel: (410) 296 0232

e-mail via www.interdys.org/ContactUs.htm

An international organisation which provides information
and services. It does not provide diagnoses, assessments
or tutoring but its website has a directory of professionals,
covering the USA, Canada and Brazil, who do. It also has a link
for tutors worldwide – www.tutors-international.com.

LD Online
www.ldonline.org

LD OnLine

WETA Public Television

2775 S. Quincy Street

Arlington

VA 22206

e-mail via www.ldonline.org/sitecontact

A guide to learning difficulties and ADHD for educators.

Canada

See the International Dyslexia Association under the 'USA' heading.

Canadian Dyslexia Association

www.dyslexiaassociation.ca

Tel: 613 853 6539

e-mail: info@dyslexiaassociation.ca

Aims to promote awareness of dyslexia in order to improve the quality of life of the estimated 5 million Canadians who have dyslexia.

Australia

Australian Dyslexia Association

www.dyslexiaassociation.org.au

PO Box 261

Varsity Lakes

Queensland 4227

e-mail: dyslexia.association@gmail.com

Operates in every state, with offices on the Gold Coast, Sydney and Melbourne. It provides full dyslexia assessments in five states: Queensland, New South Wales, Victoria, South Australia and Western Australia.

The Australian Federation of SPELD (Specific Learning Difficulties) Associations (AUSPELD)

www.auspeld.org.au

Information and bookshop at:

Dyslexia-SPELD Foundation WA

PO Box 409

South Perth WA

6951

Tel: (08) 9217 2500

e-mail: support@dsf.net.au

Provides access to a number of excellent resources for teachers dealing with learning disabilities, students with learning disabilities and parents of struggling students.

It has state associations which give information about dyslexia and the support options available in Queensland, New South Wales, Victoria, South Australia and Western Australia.

New Zealand
Dyslexia Foundation of New Zealand

www.dyslexiafoundation.org.nz

PO Box 16141

Hornby

Christchurch

Tel: (64) 3 349 6161

e-mail: info@dfnz.org.nz

Supports people with dyslexia and provides information about organisations which enable dyslexic individuals to overcome learning issues and harness their potential. Also has details for local groups that provide a chance for parents to discuss issues and strategies for their children and adults wanting to share their own experiences.

South Africa
Childpsych
www.childpsych.co.za/child/dyslexia
e-mails are listed on website

Helps people find an educational psychologist in South Africa. Has contacts in Cape Town, Johannesburg north, east and south and Overberg.

Hong Kong
Dyslexia Association of Hong Kong
www.dyslexia.org.hk
e-mail: info@dyslexia.org.hk

Aims to increase awareness of specific learning difficulties and provide support to those affected by them.

Europe
European Dyslexia Association
www.eda-info.eu
e-mail: eda-info@eda-info.eu

An umbrella organisation for national and regional associations of people with dyslexia, parents, professionals and academic researchers with members in 24 countries.

The Contributors

David Bailey CBE
World-renowned photographer, one of the most influential of all time.

Ed Baines
TV chef, restaurateur, author and owner of Randall & Aubin in central London.

Charley Boorman
TV motorcycle adventurer, President of Dyslexia Action.

Sir Richard Branson
Virgin Group founder.

Marcus Brigstocke
Comedian and actor; well-known stand-up and regular on BBC Radio 4.

Darcey Bussell CBE
Once one of the great British ballerinas, now a TV favourite as judge on **Strictly Come Dancing**.

Brian Conley
Entertainer, actor and singer.

Sophie Conran
Runs the hugely successful, award-winning Sophie Conran homeware brand, sold across the world.

Kelly Hoppen MBE
Interior designer of homes, super-yachts, French châteaux, hotels and more.

Eddie Izzard
EMMY award-winning comedian and actor; known for his distinctive stand-up routines, and acting roles including **The Riches**, **Ocean's Twelve**, **Ocean's Thirteen** and **Valkyrie**.

Mollie King
Singer-songwriter and a member of the platinum-selling girl group The Saturdays. Mollie is also a model and she curates her own fashion range 'Loved by Mollie' for the Oasis chain. She is an ambassador for Dyslexia Action.

Lynda La Plante CBE
BAFTA award-winning author, screenwriter and producer; creator of **Prime Suspect** and **Trial and Retribution**.

Kenny Logan
Rugby player for Scotland and Wasps, now runs a sports marketing and events company.

Meg Mathews

Animal rights champion and vegan designer.

Nigel McCrery

Author, screenwriter and creator of TV series including **Silent Witness** and **New Tricks**.

Steven Naismith

Premier League footballer, plays for Scotland and Everton.

Paul Nixon

Former wicket-keeper for the English national cricket team, and captain of Leicestershire Cricket Club, still working to promote the game.

Theo Paphitis

Owner of stationery chain Ryman, homeware specialists Robert Dyas and lingerie retailer Boux Avenue, known to millions for his high-profile appearances on the BBC's long-running **Dragons' Den** series.

Chris Robshaw

England and Harlequins rugby union captain.

Richard Rogers

Award-winning architect and advisor on urban renaissance to mayors and governments across the world.

Sir Jackie Stewart OBE

Three times Formula One motor-racing world champion **and** a champion shooter; now a businessman.

Zoë Wanamaker CBE

Award-winning stage, film and television actor, star of **Harry Potter**, Agatha Christie's **Poirot**, **Mr Selfridge**, **My Family** and many more.

Zelda West-Meads

Highly respected 'agony aunt' for the **Mail on Sunday's You** magazine, counsellor and formerly spokesperson for Relate.

Benjamin Zephaniah

Poet, writer, lyricist and musician.

Photo Credits

50% of royalties from the first 100 book sales will be given to Dyslexia Action, then 50% of the royalties from book sales, less the cost of expenses incurred, will be donated to Dyslexia Action. Dyslexia Action is the working name for Dyslexia Institute Limited, a charity registered in England and Wales (No. 268502) and Scotland (No. SC039177) and registered in England and Wales as a company (No. 01179975).

Other books you may find interesting

The Self-Help Guide for Teens with Dyslexia
Useful Stuff You May Not Learn at School
Alais Winton
ISBN 978 1 84905 649 6
eISBN 978 1 78450 144 0

Can I tell you about Dyslexia?
A guide for friends, family and professionals
Alan M. Hulquist
Illustrated by Bill Tulp
ISBN 978 1 84905 952 7
eISBN 978 0 85700 810 7

An Introduction to Dyslexia for Parents and Professionals
Alan M. Hulquist
ISBN 978 1 84310 833 7
eISBN 978 1 84642 527 1